Baby Bump, Cancer Lump

-a memoir of fighting cancer while pregnant-

by Stephanie R Partridge

If you have read this copyright page in its entirety-you are my kind of person. You should sit back, enjoy a treat, and give yourself a pat on the back. You deserve it. Also, has anyone told you that you are amazing today? YOU are amazing, important, and making a difference. Air high five. Oh, and please write a review! Thank you.

Baby Bump, Cancer Lump

And *Jesus* arose, and rebuked the wind,
and said unto the sea, Peace, be still.
And the wind ceased,
and there was a great calm.

-Mark 4:38

Table of Contents

PREFACE

13 September 2016

I'm the type of person who uses projects to get my mind off things. Don't get me wrong: I am not overly ambitious, I'm not a great multitasker, and I'm probably the world's most efficient procrastinator. I tend to get a lot done in every *other* aspect of my life just to avoid the task at hand. Lately, it has been emotional procrastination.

My last surgery is scheduled for next week. I should be more excited, but I don't think I can be until the surgery is finished and I am fully recovered. I want it all to be finished now: finished with appointments, finished with tests, finished with medications, and finished with doctors.

As surgery approaches I catch myself pulling away emotionally from my family. Dealing with this is too hard for me. Anticipating this final surgery takes me back to my diagnosis and to the subsequent surgeries. The voice of fear then creeps back into my thoughts, so I reach for a distraction. Maybe if I volunteer more, plan an event, decorate our new house—any of a myriad of less important tasks—then I won't have to think about the reality before me.

Distraction works for a while. I know who's who in Hollywood, the latest fads on Pinterest, the writings of mommy bloggers around the world—these things pique my curiosity and fill the portion of the brain reserved for "fill and spill" information. Disappointingly, no matter how much useless information I cram into my brain, the pain and fear caused by the notion of death, of *my* death, will never fully be diluted.

I take a quiet moment to sit and write. As I do, emotions flow out of my mind and onto the page in front of me. Writing my thoughts is healing. I see that my pain and suffering are not caused by any condition or disease; they are caused by the meddling of that evil one, Satan, who leads me down paths of misery and torment. Pain of the body is temporary; the unchecked mind brings me the greatest anguish. If I am not filled with pure and uplifting truths, I am left open to be filled by another source who is dishonest and unforgiving.

I am not afraid of death. But I want to live a life long enough to see my five boys grown into five men, full of humility, charity, and faith. A time may come when I find myself romancing fear or doubt again. I write so I can release. I find healing in documenting the fragments of my thoughts and testimony that need mending as I cope with the weight of my situation.

This is my story: one journal entry, one experience, one moment at a time. On these pages, I offer the undiluted experience of my ordeal with cancer while pregnant.

Chapter One

-The Start-

My three-year-old woke me up at 2 a.m. in tears, acting as he does after a horrible nightmare. His small, chubby hands twisted into my hair. His chin shook as he tried to speak. Wiping tears from his face, he softly whimpered, "I want chocolate." From that one statement, before my eyes fully opened on the first day of 2015, I knew it was going to be a great year filled with laughter.

Nothing about that particular year was expected to be out of the ordinary, other than our long-planned ten-year wedding anniversary cruise with friends. Brett was happy with his job. Our four boys were young, energetic, and curious, which made for a lot of chaos. The constant demands of a baby nearing two, and his three-year-old brother at my heels every step, made me feel more like a referee than a mother. Not to mention the mishaps of my older boys, only seven and five years old, keeping me busy with a myriad of activities. I think this phase of my life could simply be defined as tired and running, always running.

We started calling our youngest son our angel baby when he was a few months old. He was the first of our boys to sleep through the night in the first year of his life. I can't even tell you how many books, theories, and recommendations I tried with my babies to get them to sleep well. Nothing except about three years' patience seemed to do the trick, until our fluke youngest, who was a much-needed break from sleeplessness.

We once did the math and learned that in the first eight years of marriage, six of those years had been spent either pregnant or nursing. Most of that time survived waking three to five times a night with different children. Zombie-like grogginess got me through the day, occasionally falling asleep in the middle of a diaper change or reading a story. Most days I succumbed to drifting off mid-sentence. Sleep is essential. People go crazy without sleep. I'm pretty sure Brett and I were crazy.

We celebrated the end of our baby making days by getting a new puppy on Christmas morning, 2014. All the sleep we had been getting made us feel ambitious. With sleep, we could accomplish anything, right? We named the new furry addition Rocky. He was the sweetest, cutest, little black and white Havachon puppy. Our boys were ecstatic to finally have a dog after years of asking, pleading, begging, bargaining, etc. Particularly, our oldest son craved a puppy to love. He, on a few occasions, managed to write "**DOG**" on many grocery shopping lists carelessly left on the counter.

Training a new puppy while still maintaining routine and normalcy for the boys was a challenge, but doable. Life just seemed perfect; crazy, but perfect. The two youngest boys frequently pretended to be puppies with Rocky, hence telling my sons repeatedly to stop licking me became routine. Personal space between myself and my children became nonexistent by the time I had my third child. Nap time for the boys turned into me hiding in my room, dropping like a hot potato for a quick nap on my bed, surrounded by laundry.

With the new puppy, Christmas festivities, and starting the New Year, I had gotten off track about exercising. I resisted going to the gym in January, with all the "resolutioners," equating that with running an errand in the middle of rush hour traffic. It could wait. Doing workouts in our basement during the boys' nap times worked for the short term. I started getting really dizzy doing an aerobics video in mid-January, to the point where I had to lie on the floor and wait for the room to stop spinning. This repeated the next two days while I exercised.

Dizziness and passing out had happened to me before, during each pregnancy. The reason I didn't make that connection immediately baffles me now. After my third dizzy spell, it dawned on me that I could not recall the last time I had a menstrual cycle.

Among fruit snacks, apples, and our weekly four gallons of milk, I smuggled a pregnancy test home from the store without a word to Brett. Stepping into the bathroom and shutting the door felt like walking into a testing center to take the SAT. Regardless of the many times I have done this test, I still read the directions twice. Two lines means pregnant. There was no question. I knew before the results came in, but now I had the visual manifestation in my hands and I was scared. I love being a mom, but I had painted a picture of my life with our four sweet boys and a puppy. That was it. My expectation of the future was altered without my permission, and my brain needed to wrap itself around the idea. I buried the two-lined pee stick under some tissue and chocolate candy wrappers in the bathroom trash.

I kept the news from Brett for three weeks. For three weeks I hid our surprise baby from my other half and closest friend. Maybe I needed to work out my own feelings about being pregnant before I introduced reality to him. More than anything, I felt ashamed for feeling disappointment. So many people I love are unable to have children, and I was blessed with this surprise, yet I didn't feel joy immediately like I felt I should have.

When I finally told Brett the news he was confused. How was it even possible? I said something about the birds and the bees to lighten the mood. We accepted the statistic that 98% effective still leaves room for 2% of persistently determined swimmers.

My obstetrician ordered an ultrasound, and we were dumbfounded when told that I was at eleven weeks gestation. Through a tender mercy, I made it through almost a whole trimester without even knowing. Those extra holiday pounds were now completely justified! If I had known then that I was pregnant, I would have insisted on more turkey and chocolate pie.

A few weeks after finding out about our little human phenomenon, I began to feel intense pain in my right breast. I have had clogged milk ducts when nursing, and the sensation was the same. I placed a warm compress on it several times for a few days, and it stopped hurting. This being my fifth pregnancy, I had learned that bodies do strange things when expecting, and I mostly just need to roll with it.

My other babies were announced by calls, emails, and/or a quick status update on Facebook. Those self-induced Pinterest expectations of announcing a baby in front of dozens of people in fancy clothes, with perfect coifed hair, eating tiny fancy food on burlap napkins just didn't magically happen. People who avoid rush-hour and the gym in January don't go out of their way when making announcements. However, I had been telling people that we were absolutely done having kids, so we needed a fun, public announcement to let people know that we were happy about this surprise. We made a hyper-lapse video (the kind of recording that makes 20 minutes of normal motion show in about 20 seconds) of my hands drawing a picture of our family and how it has grown. It ended with the penciled image of Brett and I surrounded by our four boys, a dog, and my belly fully rounded. "Coming 2015. Brought to you by statistical anomalies."

February and March seemed to fly by with training Rocky, planning for the baby, school work, and our usual chaos. Chaos was embodied in the baby we once called our angel baby. Just after Valentine's Day, I caught him retrieving his Iron Man toothbrush from the toilet. Before I could grab it out of his hand, it went straight into his mouth. Why must my boys always forget to flush? That was pretty much the most disgusting thing I had seen since, well the day before, anyway. Two days after the toilet debacle, he discovered the "swing" above the table. I ran to pull his hanging arms off of that chandelier so many times for weeks. Those instances were not the only sources of repeatedly raising my heart rate. He climbed on top of the entertainment center and later into the upper kitchen cupboards, throwing several dishes to their shattered demise. (Deep breaths.) That is the month we stopped calling him our angel baby and started calling him "Destructicon." He still was the sweetest thing when not driving us completely nuts.

While getting the kids ready for church early on a Sunday morning in March, Destructicon had a giant diaper blowout that required a lot of bleach, two loads of laundry, and a shower for him and me. It was more of a kamikaze poop explosion, to be accurately descriptive. While showering, I noticed a small lump beneath the skin on my right breast. It was about the size of a marble, in the same area that I had experienced pain weeks before. I had never had a clogged milk duct harden like that, but I had no reason to believe it was anything different. I rushed to get us out the door and managed to be seated in our pew before the opening song, with all hair combed, shirts tucked in, and no one crying at least when we first sat down. Getting all four boys ready for worship by 9:00 a.m. each Sunday is a challenge, but I knew that was where we needed to be. The boys looked so handsome, I had to shoot a picture of them when we got home. Despite the mismatched socks, the growing legs, and the wiggly bodies, I loved these boys to pieces, and I began to become increasingly more excited about adding another one to our pack. That lump I felt in the shower was at the bottom of my concern list, right next to "missing sock of 2013," and "what should I make for dinner next week." I never suspected that such a small lump would bring such a big change into my life and family.

Chapter Two

-TheDoctors-

At my sixteen-week well check with my obstetrician, I mentioned my strange, hardened clogged milk duct. He did not seem worried, but ordered an ultrasound of the lump the next day. Strolling into the hospital for the ultrasound with a smile on my face and absolutely no doubt in my mind that this was just a formality, I felt confident in my good health. I was just pleased to be out of the house fully dressed with makeup on. It was not every day I got to go somewhere without kids in tow. The hospital was like a girls' night out – except it was just me, and it was day, and it was a hospital – but hey, thrills were hard to come by.

The ultrasound of the lump in my breast was inconclusive and I was told I would need a biopsy that could be done right then and there. I called Brett to let him know what was going on. The extra time needed at the hospital was an annoyance when I had people to take care of at home, and the novelty of being out without kids had worn off. Completing the biopsy immediately was actually a blessing, as I had no time to think or learn about what would be involved in a biopsy. My brief description of a biopsy is: it hurt. Bad.

After sending the older boys off to school a few days later, I was relaxing on our couch with an ice pack on my biopsied breast. Brett came down the stairs and asked if I was okay and if I needed a hug. Of course I was fine, but he looked so seriously at me that I was confused about what he was thinking. He brought his laptop to where I sat and showed me that my biopsy results were in on my online health portal. Among a lot of words I didn't clearly understand, it stated "invasive ductal carcinoma estimated size 1.3cm." Cancer.

Shock or denial set in. Maybe both. I was sure there was some kind of clerical error. Cancer was something *other*, distant people with a lot of health issues have, not me. Not ten minutes after Brett read my diagnosis, my obstetrician called me personally to give me the news and offer his support. He was incredibly calming and sincere in offering helpful advice as well as giving me straightforward instructions as to what my next steps needed to be. He had already scheduled an appointment with a specialized breast surgeon. Brett proactively wrote down everything the doctor said. I heard words but chose not to fully listen. Suddenly, at thirty-two years old, I was a little girl, lost in a conversation of big people, in a world that I knew nothing about. I just wanted someone to hold my hand.

None of this made sense. I had a plan and this was not it. After some time, I had been able to embrace my pregnancy, so I knew that I just needed to keep myself together while I worked through the reality of cancer. The world does not stop turning, no matter what obstacle is placed in front of me. The kids still needed my help completing homework, the laundry still needed to be folded, and dinner still needed to be made. I would still lock the bathroom door so I could have a moment of peace and chocolate in the dreaded five o'clock hour, and four boys still relied on my goodnight kisses.

We told the boys our news the next night over milkshakes, with a tale of mutant cells that morphed into a mean bad mutant called The Cancer Monster, who must be destroyed. The dialogue was light, but also serious. Brett and I had cried the night before after putting the boys to bed. We had cried again when we discussed how to tell them. Yet sitting in our van that afternoon, we managed to keep our fears in check and stay positive and smiling. The boys asked questions and wanted to know if I was going to die. They also asked about how cells work and what the doctors would do. For the most part, they were preoccupied with their milkshakes, but I could see in the older boys that they knew things were going to be different. When we got home there was an intense feeling in our home. Anticipation of what was to come. Fear of the unknown. Nothing could be done but wait.

Waiting is the worst part of cancer. It seemed like every step of the way I waited to meet with a doctor, waited to get a test result, waited for the next treatment plan. The worst waiting happened right at this time after getting the cancer diagnosis and before doing anything about it. I had a ticking time bomb under my skin killing me with each dividing cell. Though my doctor assured me that the baby would be fine, I still had to go about my day and attempt to sleep at night while wondering what the demon inside me was destroying at that moment.

My mind could not focus on anything other than cancer. Sometimes I struggled remembering what I was saying mid-sentence. I lay in bed for hours at night listening to Brett snore. His breathing was rhythmic and made me a bit jealous. I could not imagine ever going to sleep peacefully again. Sometimes I got up to check on each of the boys, clean the house quietly, or write. Never in my life had I felt so uncomfortable in my own skin and body. A vision of tiny, black cancer spiders crawling around inside my cells, sucking my blood, and laying eggs haunted me. I wanted to jump out of this defective form and not think about cancer again.

Meeting with the breast surgeon was substantially informative. She taught me about cancer without me having to ask, "Okay, now explain it again as if I were a 5-year-old." I diligently took notes of everything she said, even though she also sent me home with a packet of information about breast cancer, surgery, and several medications that I would need post-surgery. She referred me to an oncologist that I would meet to discuss the next step after surgery. I drowned myself in information. I read everything. I studied each medication. The exorbitant amounts of information, statistics, and possible outcomes were overwhelming. I felt like I was reading the news about a plane crash before it happened, and I was piloting the plane.

The most meaningful information that we gleaned from the meeting was not what was intended. We learned that my cancer fed on three different hormone receptors. Those (hormones) increased dramatically because of my pregnancy. Had I not been pregnant, the cancer may have grown silently for years. Had I not been pregnant, I likely would not have noticed or mentioned it to a doctor. If Brett and I would have lived the life we planned, it likely may have been a life cut short.

We didn't get the life we thought we wanted; we got what we needed for me to live. The statistically anomalous body inside of me saved my life. In that moment, I felt the overwhelming love of a real, true, merciful God who knows and understands things that I cannot comprehend.

After informing our friends and family about my cancer, we were inundated with phone calls, texts, and emails asking how I was doing. People generally reached out to Brett, because they didn't want to bother or offend me. Since I hadn't even started treatments yet, having people talk about me rather than to me made me feel like a pariah in our circle of friends. I quickly learned that cancer could be isolating, but I would not give cancer that power. I began a public journal about this ~~journey trek~~ crappy cancer. I felt that if my writing could be uplifting, I might ease concerns and connect with others while I recovered. Journaling was also the most logical way to keep my treatments and experiences recorded.

Keeping a family record had always been important to me. I have scrapbooks, photo albums, personal journals, family journals, a blog, etc. After my diagnosis, I shuttered momentarily, thinking, "Is this why I've been so good at recording everything? I'm going to die!" I was like the fat turkey on the farm, realizing what Thanksgiving is all about for the first time.

A memory only lasts as long as it is recorded. With every appointment, side effect, and demand on my body, I knew there would be many things that would be forgotten without documentation. Keeping a history of cancer treatments and the daily humdrum life with my minions was therapeutic.

Like the proverbial phrase says, you don't know someone until you've walked a mile in their shoes. Here are my shoes. Put them on. If reading my story helps you better understand the world of cancer, how to empathize with someone you love who has been diagnosed, or with your own trials, then I offer my mile to you.

2 April 2015

While sitting in the waiting room of the surgeon and filling out a million pages of medical history, all I can think is, "Man, other than four C-sections and breast cancer, I'm pretty much freakishly healthy."

My lumpectomy surgery to remove the cancerous lump is scheduled for April 15th. Three weeks after the surgery I will be okayed to begin chemotherapy. Because I am pregnant, we'll be pushing it back as long as possible, sometime in my third trimester hopefully. They'll start radiation after the baby arrives. The bad news is obviously cancer. The good news is that the baby and I will likely look like balding twins after he or she is born.

4 April 2015
Warning to everyone, this conversation just happened:
My second son: "Daddy says that if anyone makes fun of you when you're bald this summer, we can punch them in the face."
My first born: "Yeah, I'm gonna punch them in the teeth and keep all the teeth that fall out so I can put them under my pillow and be rich when the tooth fairy finds them!"
World, you've been warned.

5 April 2015
The weekend started with an old friend sending me a message. She expressed that my kids will be cared for and loved no matter what. She said even when I may be too ill to care for them, Jesus has a love for them that can reach where I cannot. He will take care of them. Her words were a tender mercy to my breaking heart.

Yesterday and today we watched the General Conference of The Church of Jesus Christ of Latter-day Saints. It was inspiring and exactly what I needed. Since finding out about my cancer, I've had many moments that have been difficult. At times, I am consumed with sorrow and mourning for my four young boys who will be put through so much. I want to take the pain away from them even though they haven't experienced it yet. I cry when I read to them at night and when my youngest, who is still a baby in my eyes, cries for me to give him hugs. I hate the thought of not being able to offer him those hugs forever.

Several of the speakers at Conference spoke about faith and not being afraid, but believing. Afterward, Brett and I had an uplifting conversation where we were able to testify to each other of our hope for the future, love for each other, and God's plan for us. I feel like my whole perspective about my situation has changed in the past two days. I know there will still be moments where I become overwhelmed, but I trust in my Savior. I believe in His infinite atonement and saving grace. I know that no matter what happens, we are in His hands, and His work and glory is to bring us joy and eternal happiness. That is what life is all about.

9 April 2015

Tomorrow we find out the gender of our baby and we are excited! Odds are in favor of a boy because that is what we know how to have, but we'll see. I met with my oncologist this morning. He seems like a thorough and experienced doctor. We went through my chemo schedule, medications, and side effects. I, unfortunately, read up on several of the possible chemo concoctions before the appointment. The nurse went over what "blend" I would be served through infusions during the pregnancy. I recognized the name immediately. Adriamycin/Cytoxan is what the cool cancer people refer to as "The Red Devil." I do not look forward to chemo, but I do look forward to being finished with it, which can't happen until after I start. Four infusions of The Red Devil doesn't sound too bad, compared to some women who require many more. After the baby is delivered, I will be switched to a different chemotherapy. I won't worry about that one yet. My oncologist said this year will be an unfortunate blip in a long, happy life. I wonder if he says that to everyone, like the dentist when they say an injection will only feel like a pinch (and then comes a ten-inch needle that feels like a punch in the jaw)? I'll focus my thoughts on being done and guessing what my hair is going to be like when it grows back. My hope is curly red hair; that would be so fun.

10 April 2015

Today was ultrasound, OB/GYN, and echocardiogram day. It was a great day! I absolutely love the staff at my office. When the nurse took me back to get my vitals, the first thing she said was that they've all been talking and thinking about me, and that I've been in her prayers. I can't imagine a more loving office environment. Now for the drum roll, please: number five is... a BOY! Taking sponsorship endorsements now from Five Guys burgers and fries. I should make some tee-shirts or something.

13 April 2015

Three weeks ago, I was asked to be a Gospel Doctrine instructor for Sunday School. I love teaching and was thrilled to have this new opportunity, so right after I was given the calling I prepared my upcoming lesson. There were three aspects to the lesson: 1. Humility: Becoming as a Child (Matthew 18:1-6); 2. Forgiveness: The Parable of the Unmerciful Servant (Matthew 18:21-35); and 3. Charity: The Parable of the Good Samaritan (Luke 10:25-37). As I prepared the lesson I wanted to focus most of the discussion on The Good Samaritan. I made an outline and left it on my computer desktop.

Then cancer came and life became crazy. The time approached to teach the lesson, so I got my notes back out. My life had changed in that short amount of time between preparing the lesson and delivering it. I became emotional reviewing my notes on how we can have more charity in our lives. I felt that I needed to completely change my outline.

Instead of focusing on charity I focused on humility and forgiveness, because I didn't think I could make it through my lesson as it was. I am stubborn and prideful, and asking for help from anyone is admittedly one of the hardest things for me to do. Yet, in the past couple of weeks I have found myself in the place of the man fallen among thieves. I cannot do it on my own. For the next several months I will have to put my trust, my life, and my pride on the table and accept the lot that I have been given.

I have been blessed to be surrounded by many Good Samaritans in my life, which makes the parable very real for me. I am blessed with an amazing husband who is willing to drop everything for me, a wonderful family on both sides, and numerous friends and neighbors who have come to my aid. I could not ask for a better support group. I know this whole process will be difficult, humbling, and at times painful, but I feel blessed to have a trial that is so apparent to everyone. My heart aches for the many people who suffer in silence from invisible afflictions. I've opened up about my situation because I'd rather be transparent than be the topic of hushed conversations and rumors. My problems will be seen clearly. Many people have far more challenging trials spiritually, emotionally, physically, financially, etc., that can tear apart who they are without anyone knowing.

Let's be kind and have charity to each person who crosses our path. We don't always see the pain and struggles people face, but they are there. I would much rather take cancer than endlessly suffer in silence from an ailment that no one understands or sees. Like the Good Samaritan, we can choose kindness over apathy, to care for and heal those that have fallen in some way.

14 April 2015

I've been told that when going through the cancer-killing process I shouldn't plan anything, because my schedule belongs to the doctors and hospital. Well, I just got a call thirty minutes ago from the hospital telling me that I need to come in now to do some lab work, an x-ray, and fill out paperwork in preparation for my surgery tomorrow. It seems like they could have told me that a week ago. I got permission to wait a couple of hours until my toddler wakes up from his nap. So it begins!

15 April 2015-morning

I'm sitting in the waiting room. Deep breath. No makeup—check. No deodorant—check. No food—check. Toddler vomiting before we left—check. Favorite hospital socks ever—check. Let's do this thing! Cancer removal begins in T minus 5...4...3...

I remember the morning of my first surgery well. After all of the research I had done on chemotherapy, the surgery seemed like a small pit stop before getting into the hard stuff. My anxious nerves did get to me that morning though. I was sick to my stomach before we left. We did not expect my son to be sick too. He threw up all over the comforter on our bed. In a hurry to get out the door, my husband pulled the comforter off the bed and took it straight out to the trash. We dropped the kids off at a friend's house and got in the car to head to the hospital. Have something dirty? Trash it. I should have used this technique when potty-training all of my boys. I could have saved hours of laundry time.

15 April 2015

I'm feeling more coherent and less drugged, glad to be done with the first step of this process: the lumpectomy. I'm so thankful for the kind words, encouragement, and help offered to us. The best part of the day was being injected with radioactive liquid for the doctors to be able to locate my lymph nodes during surgery. My boys will think I'm the coolest person ever when I tell them I'm radioactive! I may be one step closer to being boobless, but I'm also one step closer to being like Spiderman. Brett came to the hospital to be with me tonight after the kids were asleep. He told me about my oldest son's prayer before bed. He prayed that I would get better fast and then sincerely pleaded with the Lord that Dad wouldn't forget his sandwich for lunch tomorrow. Hahaha.

16 April 2015

I can go home from the hospital! I'm also just finding out that I'm not allowed to shower until Sunday. Grrr.

17 April 2015

Day two of recovery is going great. I stopped taking pain medication the night of the surgery because it made me feel like a zombie. Yesterday, I had ice on my breast and armpit all day, but today I'm free of the ice too. I'm a bit sore, but recovery is much easier than those of my C-sections (the only surgery I can compare it to). I love that I can laugh, sneeze, and cough without feeling like my organs might fall out, which is what it felt like after my babies. My arm has great movement, but I don't have muscle use in my pectorals on the right, so there are some things that I can't do, like open lids. Now I have a good excuse for not being able to open all those jars that manufacturers seem to glue shut.

My port-a-cath has been more irritating than my lumpectomy wounds, but that might be because our toddler kind of landed on it this morning, which made me tear up. I really couldn't ask for a better recovery so far, at least during the day. Sleeping is rough because I can't lie on my right side, left side, back, or front. Sleeping propped up on the couch seems to work for now, though. Brett's working from home because I can't lift anything. I call for him if the kids need to be picked up and that system is working out just fine. My whole family has felt cared for and upbeat during this process, and that makes adjusting to these changes so much easier.

18 April 2015

I got out of the house today! Two of my boys had their first soccer games of the season and it was refreshing to be out and watch them have fun. My oldest got to be goalie for a while, which was pretty funny to watch. I'm fairly certain he only wanted to be the goalie so that he could wear the cool goalie gloves. He didn't have much interest in blocking the ball. My second son loves running back and forth on the field. He kicked the ball a few times, but mostly laughed and smiled as he ran back and forth with his team. I'm all for anything that gets my boys exercising.

I have a couple of weeks before I start chemo, so I wanted to get some things chcecked off my pre-treatment bucket list before my immune system gets attacked. This includes things like being in crowds, visiting dirty and germ-infested public places, and being around other people who may be sick. A friend took the boys this afternoon, so Brett and I went to a movie (the most perfect crowded, germ infested public place we could think of). It was nice getting out, even if I haven't showered since Wednesday. I'm glad Brett isn't too embarrassed to be around me. I'm tired, but all of the activities today involved a lot of sitting, so it was a good recovering transition to normal life. Tomorrow I'm heading to church, showered and all.

19 April 2015

I wanted to make it through church without crying. I failed three times. The first cry was in the first few minutes of sacrament meeting (communion). After a few announcements, we began our meeting with a hymn I've sung hundreds of times. Most three-year-olds, in our church, know at least some of the words to this song because we teach it to our children before they can speak full sentences. I started to sing, "I am a child of God, and He has sent me here." As the second verse began, it was like I had never heard it before: "I am a child of God, and so *my* needs are great."

Sometimes I get so caught up in being the best I can be that I forget to be human is to be weak. Without weakness and faults, we will never become who God intends us to be. After all, Christ himself had His own human weaknesses. In order to become our Savior and Redeemer, our perfect example, He had to experience and ultimately overcome the imperfections of others: hunger, criticism, unpopularity, betrayal, and incomparable pain in His mortal body, to name a few. Without those experiences to rise above, how could He comprehend our pain and understand our sorrows?

This morning I read in the fifth chapter of James where Jesus said, "Confess your faults one to another, and pray one for another, that ye may be healed. The effectual fervent prayer of a righteous man availeth much." We cannot be healed without first recognizing and admitting that we are weak. Some needs are greater than others. Some weaknesses are more apparent than others, yet we all have so much in common. We are all children of a Father in Heaven, our God, who loves us, cares for us, and allows us to be weak so that in our weaknesses we can be made strong.

20 April 2015

When I talk to people, I notice their eyes looking down at this strange thing protruding under my skin below my collarbone and up my neck. I try and keep it covered, but you can still see it on my neck. Here's the thing: I was abducted by aliens and they installed a mutant alien beetle under my skin,

or at least that's what it looks and feels like. Seriously though, it is called a port-a-cath, or more commonly just "port." A port is like a small pin cushion inserted under my skin with a catheter that connects the port directly to a vein in my neck. The port is kind of creepy looking and it hurts. It seems weird to have it sitting there sticking out a half inch under my collarbone. I've been told that I will be grateful for it when I go through chemo. With the port, I won't have a constantly bruised, sore arm with needle tracks all over. They can easily stick a needle in the port and all the medicine will get to the right place. I think I will have a big party when it can finally be removed, because once the port is gone it will really feel like closure from this whole ordeal.

I haven't had a good pregnancy dream for a while, so it was refreshing to wake up this morning "knowing" that I did some much-needed retail therapy in my head and came away with six new pairs of shoes. I always have a lot of shopping dreams when I'm pregnant.

21 April 2015

I just got the tumor test results from my surgeon. They test six sides of the cancerous tumor to look for traces of cancer cells that have spread beyond the mass. Five of the six sides tested positive for cancer cell growth. Getting this bad news is not easy to hear. What this means is they will continue with chemotherapy as planned, to shrink the cancer growth and keep things at bay while I am pregnant. After my chemo treatments have been completed, they will do a mastectomy. I am stage 2B and have not received the genetics report back determining my predisposition for future cancer. We should get those results back in a week or two. By the end of the year I will, hopefully, have my reconstructive surgery and will no longer appear to have nursed four hungry boys. I'm trying to look for the positives in all of this.

22 April 2015

Brett and I met with the perinatologist today. He said the baby looks perfect. We even got a picture of the baby giving us a thumbs up. We discussed chemotherapy and the safety of having treatments while pregnant. Having chemo in the first trimester can be dangerous and cause birth defects, but having this particular chemo in the second and third trimester has been proven safe. The main concern we will face is fetal growth. Moms that have chemo while pregnant tend to have smaller babies.

It was nice seeing the baby on the ultrasound screen after surgery and knowing he is doing well. I'll be meeting with the perinatologist or OB/GYN a week after each chemo treatment, and then twice a week from 32 weeks until delivery. They will monitor the baby's growth, placenta, and stress levels. I'm not looking forward to adding more appointments to what's now looking like an extremely busy summer already, but of all of my appointments, these will probably be the happiest. No needles. No chemo. Just checking on baby.

23 April 2015

The follow up appointment with the surgeon went well this morning. Everything looks great and we made tentative plans for the mastectomy three weeks following my last chemo treatment. Two great things: I don't have to meet with the surgeon again until after the baby is born AND we'll hopefully be able to fit the chemo, radiation, mastectomy, and reconstruction surgery all in the 2015 year, crossing our fingers.

We swung by the oncologist's office to pick up my wig prescription. According to insurance claims, it is not a wig, it is a "full cranial prosthesis due to chemotherapy induced complete alopecia." Call it what you want, I'm excited to go wig shopping this weekend.

25 April 2015

Wig shopping. 1. Wig shops are creepy. 2. Nets are itchy. 3. Trying on lots of colors is entertaining!

Chapter Three

-The Red Devil-

My particular cancer is what they call a triple threat. It has three hormone receptors. The cancer feeds on and grows from estrogen, progesterone, and HER2 found in the body. The doctor's goal is to kill off the cancer's food supply (hormones) effectively putting me into early menopause. So, unlike many other types of cancer, my breast cancer treatments promise weight gain with a slowed metabolism and other common symptoms of menopause. So much for my cancer weight loss plan!

Recently, I read about ridiculously daring (a.k.a. crazy) people who sit on kayaks in shark infested waters at night and watch the movie Jaws on a floating movie screen. The sound of the music is slow at first and then increases in volume and speed as danger approaches. Duh duh duh duh duh, ahhh!

I could hear the Jaws theme music getting louder and louder in my head as my first day of chemotherapy approached. The apprehension provoked my brain with a desire to know all that I could about my cancer. The more research I did, the more fear I generated, just like sitting in those shark infested waters while watching people being eaten alive. After all was said and done, I was grateful to have done as much studying as I had, but those days at my laptop reading one horror story after another were emotionally taxing. Repeated reports from people saying they would rather die than have to go through the arduous Red Devil again was, to put it lightly, not comforting.

When my oncologist discussed my treatment plan, he said I would be having a total of eight chemotherapy infusions. Each chemo treatment built off the last, so I should expect a longer recovery for each consecutive infusion. He let me know that I should prepare for each infusion process to take six to eight hours. I could not remember ever spending that many hours away from my boys in a single day.

The side effects I had learned about included hair loss, nausea, skin or nail discoloration, extreme fatigue, mouth sores, loss of fertility, poor appetite, and low white blood counts. I also learned that it would be important to carefully diet, avoid anyone who is or may be sick, and stop eating the occasional grape or M&M that's fallen from the table. I can't be the only one who cannot resist the good stuff, no matter where it is found. Once chemotherapy began, I would need to avoid being near anyone who had recently been vaccinated, so we vaccinated our almost two-year-old early. The music was getting faster still, duh duh duh duh. . .

I had to get my mind off chemo for a while, so I checked more things off my "Pre-Chemo To Do List" that was displayed on the magnet board in our dining room. My checklist seemed long, but it wasn't too intimidating to look at since it was displayed right next to my boys' art and some brightly colored homemade magnets. I updated each of my boys' scrapbooks, made sure my wig was nicely placed on its make-shift stand (using an upside-down vase on my closet shelf), made summer journals for the kids to write their adventures in, and researched healthy diets and recipes. Having the older kids in school was nice so I could stress when they were gone, and I got a lot of stuff done while my little ones were taking naps or having their afternoon quiet time.

I've always made big plans for summer break. "Mom school," weekly field trips, and play dates were scheduled and highly anticipated by my kids. I felt like having a solid summer plan in place early made for a smoother summer with less sitting around and nagging. The boys always knew that each day we would have an educational lesson, some kind of homework, a craft or science activity, and a daily chore. Once all of that was done, the rest of the day was dedicated to running around outside with friends or going somewhere fun. The greatest guilt I felt when it came to cancer treatments was the three months of summer where the boys would be stuck in a sterile sick house with a mom who never got out of bed. The thought scared me and I wanted to do all I could to make sure they could have a happy, youthful summer.

My mom, who lived six hundred miles away, offered to move in with us during my treatments before the baby came. It was an open-ended stay offer, and her willingness to come was another tender mercy for our family. We moved our toddler out of his crib and into a big boy bed in a room with his older brother and cleared the room for Grandma. A friend loaned us a bed to put in the room just in time for her arrival on May second. The kids were so excited to have company. The first thing she did upon arrival was read The Very Hungry Caterpillar on her new bed with the two youngest boys gathered next to her lap. With nearly one hundred appointments during my time of treatments, I'm not sure how we would have functioned without her.

The night prior to my first chemo treatment, I attempted a funny poem to lighten the mood based on 'Twas the Night Before Christmas. I'm pretty sure my anticipation was similar to the intense feelings of a child waiting for Santa's coming, except my anticipation was not jolly or bearing any gifts I wanted to keep. (Don't worry, I won't be giving up my day job any time soon for writing poetry.)

6 May 2015

'Twas the night before chemo when all through the house,
Not a creature was stirring, not even our puppy Rocky (rhyming is overrated).
The prescriptions, thermometer, and lotions are ready,
In hopes to give comfort and relief when things are unsteady.
The boys are all nestled snug in their beds,
While visions of "the first chemo presents" dance in their heads.
And I in my sweats and Brett driving home,
Have been blessed to feel so un-alone.
With fear of the unknown heavy in the air,
We know we must put our trust in God for our care.
Now Colace! Now Senna! Now Imodium! Now Digestzen!
Ondansetron! On Ativan! On Phenergan and peppermint!
To the top of my bed! To the seat of the toilet!
Now cancer away! Cancer away! Cancer away for all!
Breast cancer is a beast and I want it away,
Chemotherapy is my answer to letting me stay.
We feel strengthened in prayers said in our behalf,
They will carry us over these deep waters like a safety raft…
Okay, I'm done poem-ing. I'll be real in saying that I'm scared but hopeful. I made extra time for snuggling my boys and having fun with them today.

My stomach was turning before arriving at the cancer center. With all the research I had done, I had worked this day up as some major horrific event. When we arrived, there was no loud music, no pits of despair that I would fall into. It was a nice office with energetic staff. There were several people also waiting for their cancer treatment like me, although they appeared sad and tired. We met with the oncologist first, and I had blood work done in a small room off the main hall. Hearing from my oncologist that it would be safe to hug, hold, and kiss my boys after chemo was a beautiful sound. I had read about some chemo treatments making your skin so toxic that you can't be near other people, and the thought put me in panic mode. He did let me know that my urine would turn red and it, along with my sweat and saliva, would be toxic for the first 48 hours after my infusion. I was supposed to flush twice after going to the bathroom, wash all of my underclothing and sheets after the first 48 hours, and basically avoid spitting on people.

The room dedicated to infusions in the cancer center was like a large living room. There were several recliners placed around the infusion room in a semi-circle with a nurse's desk and table at the open end leading to the hall. The walls were white with stained-glass stars hanging from the ceiling. Nothing about the room was pointedly calming or pretty, but it wasn't scary. I felt like the people waiting were watching me, the newbie. Brett and I were the only young people by a few decades and we felt like maybe we could lighten the mood in the room a bit. We talked with everyone. We smiled and laughed. Some of the sad faces lit up and smiled back. I resolved to always walk into the cancer center with a smile on my face, which I did.

We made some new friends during my infusion. I shared some of the secrets I had learned during my research, like chewing on frozen grapes while they inject the Red Devil helps prevent mouth sores. The cancer center was not all that bad. It was far from the horror thriller I had made it out to be in my mind. The first chemotherapy was anticlimactic, and I was especially grateful.

7 May 2015- after chemo

At around 2 p.m. my body started to tingle all over, and I could almost feel my blood flowing through my veins, which was a peculiar sensation. I lay down and was happy to wake up when my oldest boys got home from school so I could hand out their "first day of chemo" gifts we prepared for them. We decided to have a surprise gift for the boys every time I have chemo or a surgery. It's nothing fancy: coloring books, little toys, play-dough, etc. The gifts will be just enough of a distraction to keep them busy and help them be happy.

8 May 2015

This morning I received my first Neulasta injection. The day after each chemo treatment, I have to go back to the infusion center for this shot (Bee Sting from H-E-double hockey stick... Okay, I exaggerate, a little). Neulasta has been proven to increase the effectiveness of chemo by putting bone marrow in super drive, producing ridiculous amounts of white blood cells. I took a deep breath and kicked one of my legs up as they shot the potent drug through a needle into my upper arm. Luckily, it only hurt for 10-20 seconds, and then it was done. They said it would give me achy bones for a few days, but as long as I'm faithfully taking Claritin and Aleve, the pain should be fine.

No throwing up yet from chemo. My main issue is exhaustion and I've been having some weird/funny equilibrium imbalances. My mom drove me to the cancer center. On the way home, I had her stop the car at the elementary school so

I could give a quick high five to my boys. They were running for an activity/fundraiser on the grass field next to the main school building. I couldn't stand for long, so now I'm back home in bed.

8 May 2015

The Neulasta side effects kicked in tonight. I crashed around 5:30 p.m. on the couch. I wasn't really awake, but occasionally opened my eyes and one of my boys would be climbing on me. The bones in my back, arms, and neck feel bruised and aching. The pain is not horrible, but it is not great either. These symptoms should be gone in another day. I've been feeling like I've had it too easy, so I'm glad to get one of these symptoms done. I have a perfect distraction tonight though—movie night on our couch with Brett and my Mom while the boys are asleep.

9 May 2015

I guess today was my crash day. I feel fine now, but I was SO incredibly tired all morning. I slept in and then, after being up for a short while, I became completely exhausted and had to take another nap. I woke up around one and feel like I've missed most of the day. I'll take being tired to throwing up any day though. I am happy with how well my first chemo has gone. Since it has been 48 hours, the chemo toxins are now out of my body. I'm no longer peeing fluorescent pink.

I am grateful to be young with a freakishly strong immune system to begin with, which I'm sure will help with my recovery. It gives me a bit of an advantage at handling the chemo side effects. Playing in the dirt a lot when I was a child has become a blessing today. However, I'll now need to learn to be cautious of germs when my immune system is at its lowest function, from the fifth through tenth day post chemo.

11 May 2015

Germaphobe Day 1: On days five through ten following chemo, the white blood cells in the body go through a rapid drop and leave me susceptible to infection, sickness, and everything else floating around. With my four boys under eight years old, keeping the house free of germs will be nearly impossible, but we are doing our best. Sanitation stations have been set up by the entrances to the house. When the boys walk in they will be inundated with hand sanitizer, wet wipes, and an area to strip off anything dirty. They are starting to get used to the routine. Lots of washing hands. No sharing cups, utensils, or anything else is a hard one for kids. Door knobs and light switches are all disinfected daily. I'm still feeling pretty good. My main complaint is exhaustion. I have two-hour energy spurts throughout the day but have to get a good rest/nap in between the energy or else I feel like I will collapse. I expect this week to be my recoup week, so I look forward to gaining more energy as the week goes on.

P.S. I have realized that I have a greater fear of death in the passenger seat of the van while my mom drives than I do of cancer. Thanks, Mom, for keeping my eternal perspective in balance.

12 May 2015

Yesterday was a somber day in our home. After a mindful family discussion about expectations, responsibilities, and our sweet new Christmas puppy, we unanimously concluded that it wasn't fair to our puppy to keep him when we couldn't give him the attention and training he deserves with all the demands on our family right now. We gave him to a family that we knew would give him the attention he needs. It was not an easy decision to come to, and we will miss him dearly. We took him and the boys out to the park for a final goodbye before he went to his new home. Our oldest two boys took it the hardest. There were tears on their pillows at bedtime. I try and look for the good that has come since my diagnosis, but cancer robs a great deal and today cancer was a thief in our home.

13 May 2015

Makeup is really disgusting in relation to germs. This week I will be makeup free to avoid contamination. Also, to be cautious I brush my teeth at least four times a day.

Each day during my lowered immune system we do post homework cleanup. We all wash hands and disinfect homework areas. I also avoid books brought home from the library as much as humanly possible.

Today my in-home nurse (a.k.a. my mom) is sick. I'm not feeling great either, but I'm not as bad as she is. Taking care of things today has been kind of nice for me to feel useful. I am so grateful for people's kindness and willingness to watch my kids.

14 May 2015

Today: Bleach, rubber gloves, disinfectant wipes, disinfectant spray, essential oils, a trip to the pharmacy, and a good rain outside. I'm not the patient right now, my mom is, so I get to play nurse. . . from a distance. . . and with rubber gloves and a mask on. One week since chemo and I'm really feeling like myself again. I took a short nap/rest for an hour this morning and I've been up and active the rest of the day. Neighbors were surprised to see me out and driving around. So, I assure all those curious minds: I won't be out unless I'm feeling up to it, and be aware that cancer is not contagious! Chemo gives me good days/times and bad days/times. If I'm feeling good I'm not going to wallow in my cancer, I'm going to live and get things done. Don't be offended, however, if I don't give hugs or shake hands. I need to be germ aware right now and your germs scare me. Tomorrow I get to peek on our baby. Woohoo!

15 May 2015

25 weeks gestation and Baby is doing well. Measurements are right on track and there is plenty of fluid, so no concerns from the doctor. It is always nice to hear good news. I managed to make it through the entire hospital trip only touching the paper on my hospital bed and the tip of a pen, after which I disinfected my hands. I'm becoming a ninja of germ dodging.

Humor is my mask. If what I'm writing sounds rosy and wonderful for us, then just know that I am trying my best to keep it all together. It is important to me that I show my boys that through any affliction we can choose to find joy.

When I was about nine, my family moved across the country. It was the first hard reality experience I can remember. I was angry. While listening to the radio, I heard a cover of the song "Smile" by Charlie Chaplin. Listening to the lyrics of that song, I felt like I could get through this trying time in my youth.

Since that time, "Smile" has remained my favorite song of all time, outside of hymns. The lyrics taught me that through any trial I can smile, and eventually I will get through it. Fake it 'til you make it has been my best medicine when I just didn't know what to do or how to cope.

Being diagnosed with cancer isn't just another trial. I am fully aware that I am facing what could have been my impending doom. If I throw in some laughter along the way, I cope. Making things happy in no way is meant to diminish the magnitude of the cancerous beast within me, but it certainly is a great distractor.

16 May 2015

Six man hours of deep cleaning today. The house smells like a hospital and I kind of like it. I thought I'd share my daily health regimen. I have always felt healthy. The last time I saw a family doctor was probably two years ago when I caught strep throat. I know that chemo will take my "perfect" health away, but I am doing my best to preserve anything good in me.

Each day I take a prenatal vitamin, fruit and veggie supplements, probiotic, and essential oils. I have put myself on a diet of no sugar, soy, white flour, white rice, yams, and most all processed foods. I do this diet for ten days surrounding my chemo and when my immune system is at its lowest. After the ten days, I allow myself a few days of limited "cheating." This is something I've chosen to do based on the research I have done.

My doctors are aware of my diet and I have received praise from the choices I have made concerning my food. Today was my first cheat day. I ate a healthy breakfast, but I had a small piece of chocolate cake later. It was DELICIOUS, but did cause some heartburn and a headache. Funny how sugar does that when re-introduced to the body.

17 May 2015

I taught Sunday School today. I love learning from the comments and experiences of those in class. I am certain that I need this calling as a teacher more than anyone needs to hear from me, and I am grateful to have the opportunity. I wanted to share the end of my lesson, but ran out of time, so I'll share my thoughts here.

In Luke 17:11-19 we learn that Christ stopped in a village on His way to Jerusalem where He heard the cries of ten lepers who stood from a distance calling, "Jesus, Master, have mercy on us!" He told them to go and show themselves to the priests. They were all healed while on their journey. Once healed, one of the ten returned to give thanks to Jesus. He "fell down on his face at his feet, giving Him thanks," and Jesus then asked where the other nine were, but they were not to be found. Jesus blessed this one saying, "Arise, go thy way: thy faith hath made thee whole." Jesus is and was known for His many miracles. He healed the sick, gave sight to the blind, allowed the lame to walk, and healed leprosy, but these acts alone were not His defining moments.

Christ became our Redeemer not for lifting our worldly burdens, but for lifting our spiritual inadequacies and limitations. We are all broken, blind, and lacking when it comes to being whole or perfect and able to enter the presence of our perfect Father in Heaven. If we see God as a God of instant gratification and "easy" healing, then we do not really see Him, making us more like the nine who were healed and kept walking. It was from the one leper who returned to praise and give thanks that we are reminded that to be made whole is a far greater reward.

It is through faith and trust in Heavenly Father and His plan for us that we can overcome any obstacle or earthly inadequacy. He can make me complete. He can mend my heart and mind when I come to Him with a "broken heart and a contrite spirit" (2 Nephi 2:6-7). I am His, and He cares for His own. I need to spend more time in praise and gratitude for not only giving me worldly blessings, when He sees fit, but for giving me His Son who suffered all things so that my broken spirit can be healed.

I can't imagine going through this trial our family currently faces without the knowledge that I am in God's hands. No matter what happens, I feel the warmth of my Savior's love like a security blanket over my childlike naiveté in this world of cancer. His care will always be for our eternal happiness. He loves me more than I love myself. He loves my family even more than I can fathom. I am made whole through my merciful and kind Father in Heaven and Savior Jesus Christ.

18 May 2015

Going to eat out with the family tonight I'm bringing the basics: disinfectant wipes for table and chairs, hand sanitizer, and my own silverware. Totally normal, right? Yep, I'm a cancer induced germaphobe, but at least I'm getting out.

20 May 2015

I'm going over my folder with the results from my genetics test that came in the mail. I am not BRCA positive, which means I do not have a genetic predisposition for cancer. If I had tested BRCA positive, it would increase my chance of future cancers, and because I am young it would most likely be more than once. Being BRCA positive would also be a clear warning for the rest of my family to get tested. The BRCA gene is often hereditary. This negative test result is one big positive in my prognosis. Some women who test positive opt for preventive bilateral mastectomies. This test alone (which consisted of a small tube of blood sent to a lab) would have cost $4000 out of pocket! I am SO grateful for great medical insurance that covered most of this bill.

My hair started falling out today. Even though I knew it was coming, seeing chunks of hair in my hands is startling. I wish there was a hair fairy that would come and leave me a present in exchange for a pile of hair under my pillow tonight. It would be like a Sasquatch Fairy. That would be the best morning surprise ever!

"Thanks for the hair! Here, have a Target gift card."
Your's truly,
Sasquatch Fairy

21 May 2015

Evidently my hair loss is water activated. I didn't have any hair on my pillow when I woke up this morning (which is where most chemo patients find it). Then I got in the shower, and it was a continuous stream of hair falling on our drain trap. Just visualize a small dog resting on a bathtub drain, and that's what my hair loss looks like. I'm glad I have so much hair to begin with; I might be able to stretch this out for another day, as long as it doesn't rain.

My chemo appointment is at 12:30. I am impatient and eager. My stomach has been turning since last night with nerves. I know I've done this before, but the thought fills me with anxiety. For my next chemo, I'll push for an earlier appointment. I have homemade healthy granola, muffins, wheat bread, hard boiled eggs, and protein balls all made and ready to go for the next few days. Here we go!

21 May 2015

Chemo #2. Just chillin' in my Snuggie at the cancer lab. They tested my blood when I came in, before I started the chemo drip. The Doc says my blood work looks in range, white blood count is good, and basically everything is awesome. There are two trash cans beside me, and whenever I run my fingers through my hair I drop chunks of the hair into the trash cans so whoever cleans here won't hate me. I really thought losing my hair would be more emotionally taxing, but so far my brain is too filled with other things to worry about.

21 May 2015 (evening)

When we got home from chemo, we knew I would have about an hour or two before I crashed, so we had the boys open their second chemo presents right away. They had some time to play with their gift, and then we gathered the boys and told them we had a once in a lifetime opportunity (disclaimer: it was just our six and seven-year-old). We handed them scissors from our kitchen drawer and let them chop my hair off. This was a memorable and fun family activity. Brett finished it off just as I was starting to have a hard time keeping my eyes open. There's something about the buzz of the clippers that makes me want to snuggle into some soft sheets.

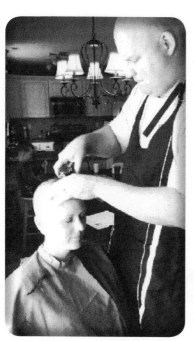

22 May 2015

Neulasta shot done. Rhogam shot done (for pregnancy because I have A- blood and Brett has A+ blood type). Woohoo! No more hospital/doctor visits till the end of next week. I like to tell a certain personal story with the nurses whenever I get my Rhogam shot, because it always makes them laugh.

When I was pregnant with my oldest and went in to get my shot, I didn't know what to expect. The nurse was nice and told me she was brand new. We went into a cubby-like space, not big enough to be consider a room, behind a curtain and she had me pull my pants down. She stuck the shot right in my bum cheek. Fast forward to my next pregnancy when it was time for me to get my Rhogam shot. The nurse asked if I knew what to expect. I confidently said I was good, been there, done that, etc. She took me behind a curtain and said she was ready, so I mooned her. She immediately advised me to pull my pants up and explained that Rhogam shots are given in the upper thigh. No pantsing necessary, just a couple of inches down

 on the thigh. I told her about my last Rhogam shot and apologized. She laughed and I'm sure I was the topic of many comical stories for her that day. Now I tell that story whenever I get the shot. Ah, laughter is good.

24 May 2015

I've nursed all of my boys. I haven't always liked nursing, and only one of my boys nursed through the whole first year, but all of them have started their lives with me being their source of nutrition. I was shopping around online, looking at baby clothing, when I came across some cute nursing covers. I was about to put one in my shopping cart when I remembered that I won't be nursing. The sting of that realization pierced. This baby will not snuggle to my breast and receive the Heaven-sent elixir of life. Any milk I produce will only last for a few days before I start chemo again and will carry toxins on to the baby.

I broke down to tears. I never thought not nursing would be a struggle for me, but the thought reminded me that this time will be different. I know that cancer isn't my fault, and to even imagine myself thinking that seems asinine, but occasionally Brett has to remind me not to put myself down because of something cancer has taken from me.

When mentioning this to a friend she offered to pump her excess milk for my newborn. She is an angel. She is providing something that cancer has stolen from me, and I will never be able to fully express my gratitude. I know that some people may think using another woman's milk is eccentric, but to me there is no greater offering. This world is filled with so many people who follow the example of the Savior and show charity, love, and kindness in all that they do, and I think it ought to be known.

26 May 2015

Not to brag or anything, but I haven't shaved under my arms for five days. Still so soft and smooth. Chemo perk.

27 May 2015

We're checking on baby this morning at the doctor's. All is well and looking good. School will be out this week for my kids, so our schedule is busy with parties and programs. Fun, fun, fun!

28 May 2015

Diagnosis: chemotherapy-related cognitive impairment or cognitive dysfunction. It is often referred to as chemo brain or chemo fog. I feel alert and on top of things most of the time, but there have been some incidences where a conversation happened and later I have absolutely no recollection of the conversation.

Occasionally I forget words, names, and other random information I wouldn't normally forget. Absent-mindedness is a common side effect of chemotherapy. Sometimes rehabilitation can take years, but being young I can expect a faster recovery. At least that's what I've heard.

If I look confused when you bring something up that we had already talked about or forget something that seems weird for me to forget, I promise I'm not trying to leave you hanging or ignoring you. I don't want anyone to treat me any differently, but just be patient.

In other news, I'm thinking that baldness is really pretty fabulous. I'll work on writing a list of why the world should all be bald... that is, if I remember.

29 May 2015

Today we hit a milestone: out of pocket max through our insurance has been reached! We have been so blessed with our insurance and we also see God's hand in inspiring us to change up our finances when the year began, before I found out I was pregnant and had cancer. Sacrifices have been made, but we are doing just fine and we are grateful.

My heart and empathy goes out to those who have to go through this AND deal with the stress of paying a single bill that is more than $17,000 without help from insurance. I am amazed and shocked at the cost to fight cancer, and I am so glad that we are finished for the year. I am also incredibly glad to be married to a man who has taken care of every bill and dealt with the insurance and hospital so I won't have to worry about it. I feel extremely blessed! Oh, and after some number crunching and estimating on future surgeries based on the previous, we are estimating the cost for this year's expenses (if it was all out of pocket) would be about $200,000!

31 May 2015

Bald privilege #1: I just showered, brushed teeth, got fully dressed, did my makeup, and wrapped my headscarf. It took me 15 minutes! Seriously! If we just explain that by shaving our heads we will never be late again, maybe men will stop complaining that women take forever to get ready. We could actually get ready faster than men can. Taking a long time is not because we are women! It is because of hair! I think this is the best part of no hair. The only problem I've noticed is using too much face wash. Without hair, I don't know where my face ends, so my face and up to my ears ends up getting a good wash every night. My bathroom counter is covered in water by the time I'm done. My bald husband and I had a good laugh about my face washing predicament.

31 May 2015

I checked on the boys tonight in the dark, pulling sheets over shoulders and picking up legs and arms that had fallen to the sides of their beds. There were a few action figures and Legos that I picked up so they wouldn't step on them in the morning. They lay so peacefully. I never wanted to introduce them to such a heavy thing like cancer, so young.

Earlier, when I read to them, I started crying and had to stop the book when the pages became blurry. I hope they don't remember all the times I have cried in front of them over the past few weeks. I am afraid of missing out. The cancer doesn't scare me as much as not being here to give the baby a hug and kiss on his first day of kindergarten. Not being here to be the one to tell the boys that junior high is kind of awful but high school is better scares me. Not being able to give them advice when they move away from home, or waiting impatiently by the door when one of them comes home late from a school dance, or not being around to meet who they choose to marry scares me.

Motherhood is a great work where every aspect of creationism is employed, and I treasure this difficult work that I do. My children are the pinnacle and masterpieces of my creative life, my greatest accomplishments, and my greatest fulfillment. I wish I were a better mom each time that I yell or spend more time getting stuff done rather than stopping to cherish the little fingers that hold mine and the nonsensical stories that never end. I want more time to become a better mother.

Sometimes my brain takes me to the worst-case scenario. Just after being diagnosed, I would hop in the van to listen to music and cry. I would have to pull over to the side of the road just to sob. I wondered if my destructicon we now call "Bubba" would remember how I shower with him in my arms and we fill our cheeks up with water to spit on the shower wall and laugh. He is too young. He won't remember if I'm gone.

Will they remember that whenever I held their hands I squeezed it three times and said "I love you?" I cried when I thought about missing countless life events and milestones. I cried when I thought about them not having my shoulder to cry on when they have heartache, when they get hurt, when they feel alone. Would my baby survive this? I worried about Brett. He doesn't know how to run the house by himself, to take care of the boys' schedules and appointments, to make sure the boys are brushing their teeth.

There are times and moments when my mind wanders to a dark place. I do my best to hide my fears from my boys. I don't want them to be afraid, like me. I am trying to not feel sorry for myself. Brett and I both mourn in our own way. Sometimes we mourn and council together, but Brett is always the rock in this. He has given me perspective and comfort. After staying up talking late a few weeks ago, I fell to my knees in fervent prayer to my Father in Heaven asking for peace and understanding. I also asked Brett to give me a [1]priesthood blessing. Almost immediately, I felt the love of God for me and knew the answers would come.

Over the next few days, I felt the Holy Ghost filling my mind and heart with a completely altered view of my situation from what I had found myself in previously. It was as if the storm and chaos in my life was completely gone. The cancer was still there, but it had no power over me. Just like Christ calming the waters in a storm and demanding, "Peace, Be Still!" He demanded the doubt, fear, anger, and stress to be still within me. I don't know how I ever allowed myself to give in to doubt.

I have every confidence that I am in God's hands. If I die, I die in the arms of my Savior. If I live, I live in the arms of my Savior. He is my shepherd, my strength, my hope, and my salvation. I am His. He is my vine and I am His branch. I will be His vessel to bring about His plan, in whatever way that may be. I know that He loves me more then I love myself, and He loves my family more than I am even capable. He will do nothing but bring about our salvation and eternal happiness when we allow Him to lead us and as we conform ourselves to His will.

In John 15:4, Christ says, "Abide in me, and I in you." I cannot think of a safer, happier place to be. Just as a newborn helplessly depends on its parents to protect, feed, care for, and raise him/her, we also are like helpless children in this life needing protection, care, and nourishment. When we abide in Christ, He will not lead us astray.

---

1. For more information about Priesthood blessings go to mormon.org

I know whose I am. I know who's got me covered. This will just be a short hardship in a long life filled with opportunities to become a better person. If this is what it takes to be "pruned" into a more fruitful servant of God, then I will take it, gladly. I want my boys to know and see that. I am strengthened and renewed by the many prayers in my behalf.

1 June 2015

Bald Privilege #2: No sweaty neck and head on a hot day! I'm feeling the breeze and looking at all those poor women with tons of hair and thinking how hot they must be. There's a reason animals shed in the summer—hair is HOT!

3 June 2015

Tomorrow is chemo #3. My mom and I did prep today: meal planning for post chemo (healthy muffins and quinoa breakfasts pre-made), healthy dinners planned for me, Costco trip (cleaning supplies, stock up on basics), pre-made frozen green smoothies in baggies. I made sure the boys' "third round of chemo gifts" are ready (they started getting excited and asking about this days ago). Most importantly, I planned a fun activity with the boys when they wake up.

Chemo doesn't scare me now that I know what to expect. I plan on being wiped out for about a week with random bursts of energy that will last anywhere from fifteen minutes to a couple of hours. I sleep and rest a lot. If I am too active (sometimes that means walking to the mailbox, other times I can walk around the block), I get really dizzy and exhausted. I love that I can still snuggle with my boys, join the family for dinner, and read books to the kids. I am grateful that my mom takes care of basic home tasks so I can spend all of my "energy time" with the kids rather than worrying about laundry or cleaning. This would be a hard place to be without such a strong support team.

One of my favorite things about spending so much time in bed is being able to look at my walls. A group of amazing women and girls I am blessed to call friends, along with my amazing husband, came to my house while I was having my lumpectomy and covered my walls in pictures, quotes, and pink ribbons that make me smile. I am truly blessed.

4 June 2015

Chemo #3: What I bring to the cancer center: frozen grapes, green smoothie, iPad and headphones, book, Brett, and blanket or Snuggie. Doc says my white blood count is perfect, platelets are perfect, and my anemia is mild, indicative of pregnancy more than effects of chemo. One more Red Devil and then on to the next drug after baby comes.

4 June 2015

Chemo is different for each person and their needs. The story, side effects, things that "work," etc. will be different. By sharing my play-by-play, hopefully it will help someone else who is going through chemo and needs a buddy.

I've had a few people ask to see my balding head. I don't mind, it's not a weird question. I'm still losing my hair in patches. Every day the patches get bigger. I am lucky that I'm not emotionally attached to my hair. I know this can be traumatic for a lot of people, but I think the whole process is fascinating.

My 'pokey' hair is like sandpaper and sticks to my pillow, so I'll need to shave it again soon. My head kind of looks like the globe of an unknown world. I think we'll call the smooth peach skin "water" and the patchy dark hair "land". In another week, I'm pretty sure the "land" will all be covered in ocean.

Chemo went well today. I've already taken a nap. I keep having random hot flashes and my body feels incredibly heavy and tired, but my brain is awake now and my phone is light, so hello social media!

5 June 2015

What a difference a day makes! My face felt scratchy on my pillow this morning from all the stubble that fell out on my pillow case. I'll just have Brett shave my remaining hair patches off tonight so my scalp is not itchy. Brett and I make quite the pair. I have no hair on my sides and he has few hairs on the top. It has been fun to watch my hair-loss process.

After chemo yesterday I had two contractions. I've been attentively aware of the baby's movements, just to be safe. My OB/GYN says to monitor the contractions. I'm seeing my perinatologist on Tuesday, so I'm not worried. I also had my first numb arm (chemo side effect) last night. I lost all feeling in half of my right arm for about a half hour. It was weird—not painful, just weird. Neulasta (bone marrow boost) shot was done this morning. I completely forgot to take my Claritin (helps with my bone aches caused by the drug) until later, but so far I'm doing all right. Resting and naps are on the schedule for the day.

8 June 2015

I feel like a blob and don't want to move. Baby will be 29 weeks on Friday, so I figured it was time to get this baby man some clothes. I absolutely love baby clothes; they are SO stinkin' cute! I'm excited to see our little guy tomorrow at the perinatologist's office.

Looking at clothes online makes me feel normal. It reminds me of my other pregnancies and all the excitement and anticipation I felt for them to come. I feel like other pregnant women don't want to talk to me. I know my situation is unique, but sometimes I want to feel like a mom who can complain about how big my belly is getting and how uncomfortable it is to bend over. Sometimes I want to think about baby announcements or about what cream I should use to prevent stretch marks. Having a petty conversation about things that don't matter would make my day. I never knew that would be something I would miss.

9 June 2015

The perinatologist appointment went well. Every measurement of my fluids and the baby were given a "perfect" report. We discussed the delivery at 37 weeks and chemo treatments surrounding delivery. My oncologist wants me to start chemo back up a few days after the baby is born, but the perinatologist wants me to have a two-week recovery break after the C-section.

I would be happy to have more time to snuggle before chemo starts again, so let's hope they fight out a good compromise for me. I try hard to focus on what's most urgently ahead of me, because thinking too far ahead can be depressing. I was reminded of my year of Herceptin injections after the baby is born and five years of anti-hormone pills. Can I just say that having menopause in my thirties does NOT make me happy? I guess if it keeps me alive and the cancer away, that's what I need to focus on.

When we got home from my appointment, my boys had bike and wagon rides. They are so cute and I am so blessed. Oh, I almost forgot! According to the ultrasound the baby has more hair than me!

12 June 2015

The itchiness of the wig is totally worth it to go and do a fun activity with the kids without getting lots of questions and looks of concern. Today I am feeling good; I'm just a hugely pregnant woman with her boys at a museum. I LOVE good days! We went to a special children's exhibit. The boys loved having me out and with them. They were a bit clingy, but I welcomed their touch. I know that they are coping with a lot right now too. I can't imagine what must be going on in their minds.

My two oldest boys are leaving tonight to stay with their Grandma and Grandpa for two weeks in Arizona. I'll be honest, I think I'm more nervous than they are. I will miss them so much. They've never been away from home without us.

They went on their first ever practice sleepover this week. Putting aside the separation anxiety I already have, I know that this will be a good experience for them. I will try hard not to completely become unhinged when we say our goodbyes. They get frustrated on my tired week after chemo when I'm in bed all the time. They will love spending time with cousins, going to swim lessons, and getting to stay with "Grandma and Grandpa Pool," as they call them.

I wasn't going to post about this, but I felt like this wouldn't be a true picture of my cancer experience without mentioning it. Last Sunday (three days post chemo) I felt like I would be well enough to make it to the first part of church. I knew I wouldn't have energy to wrestle the kids, but I could sit out in the foyer and listen. About ten minutes into it, I started to get really hot and began sweating. The room was looking warped and like it was moving, so I knew I needed to lie down somewhere. I stood up and made my way to the nearest classroom. I was so glad it was empty. I immediately went to the ground and the space around me went black for a few minutes. When I woke, my head was covered in sweat and the room was spinning. I didn't feel like I could move, so I lay on the rough carpet and cried. My mind was panicking, thinking how many germs were on the floor and how I would need to rub sanitizer all over my face when I got home. I ended up on the floor for about thirty minutes until I felt stable again.

I sat up and waited five minutes to make sure I was balanced, and then got up and went home without a word. My mom was with the boys in the pew, and I texted Brett (who was sitting up front) to let him know what happened. It was scary. I feel fine sometimes, and other times barely doing anything will make me collapse. The only sure bet is that I have one week that is an unpredictable and tired week and one week where I feel completely normal. Then it starts all over again. After last Sunday, I recognized that I should not attend worship services right after chemo. I will likely only attend the last hour so I have rest time between getting ready and actually going. I am so grateful for good/normal days and for prayer. Next Thursday will be my halfway-through chemo milestone!

13 June 2015

The hubby and I went on a nice date night to do some shopping and eat out. I am so in love with him. He doesn't give me a hard time about refusing to touch public doors or the menu at the restaurant. But, he really wanted me to pull my wig off when the waiter was talking to us for shock value. Nope. Not gonna happen. Now we're back home and I'm able to put on my pajama pants and let down my hair. Actually, I just take off my hair-much easier.

15 June 2015

I'm getting a head start on chemo prep this week. My mom and I thawed and cleaned out our freezer this morning, then I went to Costco to stock up for the next month and pre-made a dozen green smoothies that are now nicely frozen. It is a great day. I LOVE being fully stocked and organized. This next chemo will be my last Red Devil! I am so relieved to know that there is an end in sight. I want to celebrate being finished with phase one of chemo and focus all of my attention on getting ready for our baby to come.

Chapter Four

-The Void-

Unmet expectations cause turmoil. I was shocked to learn about my cancer, but my first thoughts were not "okay, let's fix this and move on." My first thoughts were "I don't have time for this. What about our anniversary cruise? What about Mom School this summer?" My initial anger and fear didn't come from the cancer itself, it came from my life expectations being altered without my consent.

When I went to the cancer center on June eighteenth, I was happy to celebrate my last Red Devil treatment before the baby came and my half-way mark for being finished with chemo. This was a big milestone of relief.

When the oncologist came in to my pre-chemo checkup room, we were told that he would be adding two more Red Devil infusions before the baby came. There was too much of a time lapse between treatments while we were waiting to deliver the baby, and my cancer was just too aggressive to let it sit untreated for that long. I have never felt more discouragement than I felt in that moment. Going in so happy, and then being given that news was devastating.

I smiled as I talked with my cancer friends in the infusion room, but I felt shattered and broken inside. I let the chemotherapy poison sink into my veins and closed my eyes to rest and process the thought of two more. I had remained positive through my other chemotherapies, knowing that this was the end, but suddenly I wondered if treatments would ever stop. Brett tried to encourage me. He reminded me that the doctor said he would schedule more space between these next two Red Devils so I would have more recoup time. That wasn't enough to make the change acceptable.

Each chemo had gotten "heavier" for my body, but this treatment was by far the heaviest. The mental weight that I carried made recovering harder. I was so exhausted. The tremendous fatigue is hard to describe. Brett had his arm around mine after the infusion. I was worried I wouldn't make it to the car. He helped me into the house and carefully up the stairs and into bed. Sleep. Sleep is all I could do to keep from breaking completely apart.

I was glad that my oldest boys didn't see me like this. Having them at their grandparents' helped ease the guilt of being an absent parent. For several days after this Red Devil treatment, I just slept or lay in bed. My mind was so busy, but my body couldn't keep up. Sometimes, just lifting my arms to change the channel of the TV felt like a workout. I would carefully prop my phone up against my big pregnant belly so I could text my mom if I needed water or something to eat. Some nasty side effects were causing me so much pain that even getting up from bed became difficult. The door to my room had to stay shut all the time so the little boys wouldn't climb on me.

In the fatigue and emotional setback from the added chemotherapies, my mind became susceptible to the adversary's reach. I was teasing the idea that maybe my doctors didn't know what they were doing. Maybe the cancer was worse than they were telling me, and I was actually dying a drawn-out painful death.

Satan, that cunning devil, knew my name. His reaches began as a simple, doubtful thought. Another thought would build upon that one, adding more doubt and more fear. Unsubstantiated information persuaded me to believe in things that were not true. The light in my hope slowly faded into gray darkness, where truth was confused with speculation and fear was my motivation.

I never knew what it felt like to be desperate until then. I felt like I was drowning, grasping for anything and everything to get me out of this pain. I feared death as the enemy, even though deep down, I knew that death was not the end. My brain felt so full of questions, speculation, and fear; so much so that simple tasks like breathing became difficult. Breathe. One breath at a time. In and out. Then fear came again because the air is full of germs.

I took the bait, feeling like my body was failing me. This body that I had trusted my whole life was not what I thought it was. This body that gave me mortality. This body that gave me my children and nourished them as babies. This body that had built a family and life was now threatening to take it all away. How could I hate my body so much? How could I hate this gift from God and see only a broken, scarred mass of betrayal?

Gray. Satan is not in black and red robes, he is in all that is gray, almost invisible and sneaking about. He snuffs out the light when the wicker is weak, swaying by the blows of the wind. He reminded me that I am weak, and whispered to me that my weaknesses could never be fixed. He reminded me that this gift, my body, was broken. He told me that my doctors lied and my suffering would not end. The devil knew me and I felt gray. I wrote these words during that time:

Hate is weak and passionate
with a loud voice to shout out its demands.
With greater fear and doubt fueling its flame.
Hate doesn't forgive.
Hate sees through eyes filtered with lies.
Hate is the call of Satan, disguised as a cause (for freedom
or truth).

Love is quiet and strong,
passionate at times,
subdued by endurance and loyalty.
powerful beyond earthly understanding.
Love is peace, empathy, and acceptance.

I hate cancer: the way it makes me feel and think, the time it has robbed me from my family, the waiting, the uncertainty. More than that, I hate that I feel this hatred. Joy seems so distant. I am trying to quiet the shouts of anger to feel that love. I love my Creator, and hope to understand how I could be made so flawed. My grip is weak, but I will hang on.

I turned to my Father in Heaven in humility. I needed to repent. I needed to ask for His help in vanquishing the evil thoughts in my mind that were riddled with hopelessness and fear. I had opened a door to Satan that never should have been opened. I could not shut him out alone, but I knew that with God's help, I could. The answer to my prayer did not come suddenly. It came in strands of hope and peace, a little at a time.

Almost a week after chemo, I had been in bed most of the day not feeling well, but I wanted to see my little boy. I got out of bed and read with him for a while until I became exhausted. I asked my mom to take over so I could go back to bed. My Bubba cried and held on to my legs, hitting me over and over again with his tiny fists clenched. He yelled at me and I just stood there. I wanted to explain to him that I was sick and needed to take a nap, but I just stood there crying. I hated that I wasn't feeling well. I hated that I was too weak to pick him up, and I felt like I deserved to be hit. He had every right to hate me right then. I hated what cancer had done to me, too. I wanted to be beat and broken just like I felt inside.

I went into my room, shut the door, and cried into my pillow. I cried more and more as I could hear my sweet little boy crying for me on the other side of the door. I wished I could hold him, walk him to the park and chase him in the grass. I wanted to be his full-time mom again. I wanted to walk away from chemo and cancer and never look back.

The cliché idiom that when God shuts a door, He opens a window, came to mind after my emotions had calmed down. An inspired friend of mine had invited my family over for dinner that night. I considered canceling after my emotionally raw day, but felt like we should go so that I wouldn't feel guilty for holding my family captive any more that day. When the time came to go, I changed out of my pajamas and chose to make the best of the rest of the day. The two boys that were home were excited to get out of the house together as a family. When we arrived, we were surprised by an army of children with poster signs of support and a slew of people wearing pink t-shirts with the text #teampartridge transcribed on the front. Several of my friends were preparing to run a half-marathon for breast cancer awareness in my honor.

They overwhelmed me with love, encouragement, and hope. My family in Arizona even video-chatted, also wearing their pink shirts to show support. I could not have hoped for a better ending to the day. It was a generous strand of hope that helped me remember that I am loved. Heavenly

Father does answer prayers, not always in the way we expect or the timing we desire, but He wanted me to know that He was listening.

Another tender mercy came through a vivid dream I had one night. In my dream, I was young and in school. The school was prestigious and I just knew it was an honor to be there. I was sitting in class when the principal called me into his office. I looked around the office and noticed the beautiful, intricate woodwork of a large desk in the center of the room. The artwork on the wall was vibrant and beautiful, and sunlight was shining through a large window at the end of the room.

Behind the desk were the kind, blue eyes of the school's principal. I knew in my heart that he cared about each of the students in the school and wanted all of us to succeed. He told me that in order for me to excel in this school, I would need to accept a difficult challenge. I was told that my opportunity for growth came in the form of being attacked by a bully every other day for the rest of the school year (definitely not what I was expecting him to say). I would get knocked down, pushed, and beaten, but the next day I could heal and enjoy my school day. Then the bully would come again.

I couldn't believe that this was required for me to succeed and become the student that he knew I could be. Why would I have to experience pain? Couldn't there have been an easier way? But I trusted him and his experience, so I agreed to the challenge, not fully comprehending what a beating would entail. As I stood up, about to leave the office, he stopped me and added that there was one more thing he needed from me. I was to be given five new students who would be under my stewardship. I would need to show them around the school, teach them how things worked, and prepare them for their coming school year. They would watch me and needed to know that my challenges wouldn't keep me down. They needed my strength and courage to confidently guide them in this new school.

In my dream, I then appeared on the playground, ready to face the bully for the first time. I looked up to see the eyes of my five new students watching me, waiting for my reaction. I knew that I was going to be fine. The bully would beat me down, but I would always be able to get back up. It wouldn't last forever. I knew that this painful challenge would help me recognize my own strength and expand my understanding of the Atonement of Jesus Christ.

When I woke up I felt contentment. I knew that this dream was a gift from Heaven to teach me that my Heavenly Father's plan for my family was better than my plan. My expectations of life meant nothing compared to the greater plan in store for me. I knew that Heavenly Father would strengthen me for my soon-to-be five boys.

It was clear that this life of mine was so small. My expectations of the future were so unimportant. Happiness in life is not about what I want. It is not about what I think I need. This mortal existence is not about being whole and perfect all the time. Happiness and wholeness in life is about taking my broken heart, my weaknesses, and my fears and turning to the Redeemer of my soul. I needed to allow Jesus to mend and fill where I was empty and broken. Then if I became broken again, I could lift myself up and start over, again and again. Jesus Christ is not a one-time Redeemer. He is our eternal Lord that always, ALWAYS lifts us up, no matter how many times we fall or how deep and lost in the darkness we become.

Elder Dallin H. Oaks, a member of the Quorum of the Twelve Apostles, said,

"Adversity is an occasional or even a constant companion for each of us throughout our lives. We cannot avoid it. It is a reality—and indeed one of the purposes of mortal life. What is important is how we react to it. Will our adversities beat us down, or will we go forward relying on the promise of God, who does not shield us from every adversity but who gives us the guidance and strength that make it possible for us to endure and progress?" (Dallin H. Oaks, "Life's Lessons Learned", Deseret Book Company, published 9/27/2011, with permission).

To rely on the promise of God and move forward would take patience with my situation and patience with myself. I turned to the scriptures to one who exemplified patience in affliction and read Job's story. In the first verse of the book of Job we learn what kind of man he was: "There was a man... whose name was Job; and that man was perfect and upright, and one that feared God, and eschewed evil" (Job 1:1). He was given every blessing and privilege in life. Satan challenged his obedience and perfection, saying that if all the good in his life was taken away he would curse God.

Jesus allowed Satan to have power over all that Job had. He destroyed his flocks and herds, he slayed his servants and his children, cursed him with boils, and abandonment and more afflictions than any one person could imagine enduring. He persevered, and despite all that he suffered he still testified, "Blessed be the name of the Lord" (Job 1:21). Job trusted the Lord and His infinite wisdom AND he accepted the Lord's will with patience and gratitude. He was declared perfect, not because he had a perfect life, but because he never doubted God's wisdom.

Patience in affliction is the opportunity to humble ourselves and open our hearts and minds for receiving the Lord's guidance and understanding, rather than fulfilling our limited expectations. President Uchtdorf wisely taught,

> "Without patience, we cannot please God; we cannot become perfect. Indeed, patience is a purifying process that refines understanding, deepens happiness, focuses action, and offers hope for peace" (President Dieter F. Uchtdorf, "Continue in Patience," April 2010 LDS General Conference, with permission).

I know, now more than ever, that Jesus Christ is my Savior and Redeemer. He suffered all things and can truly empathize with my pain and sorrow. I needed to recognize my weaknesses and acknowledge that I was broken in order to get fixed. The Savior of us all stands with open arms ready to repair each of us. I have felt His love and have a hope for peace. When we embrace the Savior, we can gain for ourselves His perfect love, perfect peace, perfect hope, and perfect forgiveness.

30 June 2015

This cancer disturbance began just three months ago. It has been a whirlwind of appointments, emotions, prayers, with some fun along the way too. There's a long road ahead of us and the mastectomy will be a beast. I'll deal with that later. I'm feeling like myself today, which always makes it easier to deal with physical and emotional strain. Even though I didn't get a full week of feeling good this time around, I'm going to do my best to enjoy the next two days before my next round of chemo.

I was invited to join an online support group that is made up of other women who are or have dealt with cancer while pregnant. Isn't that amazing?! (Not that I'm happy other people have cancer, just happy to be with people who understand.)

I was kind of giddy reading through the support group page where I saw just over one hundred women from around the world who are a lot like me. The best part is seeing dozens of pictures of mommies with their healthy "chemo babies" after cancer treatment, doing well. I'm feeling grateful today for these pictures of hope.

1 July 2015

Final five weeks of pregnancy! Time flies, especially when you don't know that you're pregnant until the end of the first trimester. This has by far been my easiest and fastest pregnancy, well, minus the whole cancer junk. Maybe the pregnancy just seems easier because I've had so many other things to worry about. The baby has been doing perfectly thus far. For the last stretch, they'll be monitoring the baby a lot more.

Today I'm starting with a non-stress test (NST: they monitor the baby's motion, heart, and mostly oxygen levels while in motion and at rest to make sure he is where he should be). After this, I'll head straight to an ultrasound to get the baby measured and check fluids, then off to see my OB/GYN. Oh, and did I mention we're celebrating two of my boys' birthdays today? This combined party is going to be so fun. We planned a big water fight with water guns, water balloons, and a slip and slide. I have to enjoy the good days to the fullest when I have them.

2 July 2015

Once upon a time, Heather and Stephanie were just two young women in beauty school together, learning the art of hair. Thirteen years later, we found one another again – this time both bald and at the cancer center getting chemo. Funny irony. Today was a fun day at chemo with lots of talking and telling stories. One lady was on her last chemo and another was on her first. I love it when there are people to talk to and laugh with during treatment.

2 July 2015

I'm not happy about having two extra chemos added to my treatment plan, but it is what it is, and we want what will give me the best odds. I put a smile on my face and took my second to last Red Devil.

In better news, the OB/GYN moved the delivery date up, so the official baby delivery day is scheduled for August 7th! I'm getting excited, and I'm also really happy to have three weeks between these next two chemos. That means more recovery time and more fun time with my kids.

Chemo hit me in the last five minutes of infusion. My eyelids, arms, and legs became very heavy. As soon as we got home I crawled up the stairs one by one and climbed into bed. I'm so grateful that Brett took our sleigh bed apart so our mattress could lie on the floor. Climbing in and crawling out is so much easier now. I've spent only an hour out of bed today.

Extreme fatigue feels like an uncontrollable, body enveloping, exhaustion. My vision has been going in and out today too, so I can't focus on much. The good news is that I'm on Season 8 of Friends... probably not something I should be proud of since I started just a couple of months ago. Yesterday, we had a water fight outside with the boys, celebrating two birthdays. Today I'm a human blob. Life is fascinating. The worst of the fatigue is usually for the first two days and then it gradually wears off. I just need to hang in there until it goes away.

6 July 2015

My mom is getting ready for a family reunion in southern Utah, so she will be gone for a couple of weeks. Today is the first day on my own, post chemo. I know being here has been hard on my mom. She misses my dad. She's thinking that when she gets back she will stay until I have recovered from delivery.

My neuropathy has faded away today, which is great. These last two chemos have given me crazy tingles and burning in my hands and palms. I was given some recommendations that will hopefully help with later chemos and to prevent further nerve damage. I think I'm recovering pretty well after this one. I'm still really tired and a bit sore, but doing well. I have a lot to look forward to this time around, because I get a three-week breather before the next treatment. More time for the body to recover is great, and I am so happy for this extended break time.

I am incredibly grateful for kind friends and neighbors who are taking my boys this week so I can get naps and rest. Mowing our lawn, bringing meals, dropping off notes, sending me an uplifting message, donating breastmilk, playing with my kids, running for a cure, and all the prayers are felt and appreciated, and they strengthen us daily beyond measure. These "small" acts of kindness mean so much to my family, more than I can express. Asking and accepting help has been hard for me, but I'm getting to be more okay with it. The sooner I get better, the sooner I can return the kindness.

8 July 2015

I just woke up from a nap to the sound of my two-year-old also waking from his nap. I wake up slowly; he wakes up playing Duck, Duck, Goose in his crib with his stuffed animals and laughing. I wish I had his enthusiasm for waking up.

I'm sure this is way too much information, but after each of my chemo treatments, I've been getting hemorrhoids and yeast infections. They have gotten progressively worse, especially with the last two treatments. I was in so much pain last night that I barely slept. Getting moving this morning was also a struggle.

I was late to an ultrasound because I passed out on the way. Brett saw me struggling before he left for work and was able to stay and help out for the day. He drove me to my appointment and pulled over to the side of the road while I came back to life after passing out. He bought me some orange juice and a muffin in a drive-through. I don't like being the cause of him missing work, but I was glad he was with me. The ultrasound went well. Baby looks good and is measuring average, which is comforting. Let's hope this feebleness of mine passes quickly.

9 July 2015

It is hard to fully appreciate nose hairs until you don't have any and you get a cold. It's unbelievable how useful those little hairs are.

12 July 2015

I consider myself blessed to be a member of my church. The Good News is taught and I am enlightened to learn a greater understanding of who I am and what my purpose is in life. I believe in Jesus Christ who is my Savior and Redeemer. He descended below all things to fulfill His promise to our Heavenly Father. He was mocked; He mingled with sinners and politicians and always remained true and faithful to His purpose. He is and was unchanging, perfect, our example, our friend, and our hero. He did for us what we in no way could do for ourselves at great personal pain, anguish, and torment. He had the power to put His agony to rest, but He chose the pain and the bitter cup so that we would not have to drink it. He spent every moment thinking beyond Himself, serving and teaching others. I hope to be more like Him and follow in His footsteps as best as I can. President Thomas S. Monson beautifully says:

> "We need not walk by the shores of Galilee or among the Judean Hills to walk where Jesus walked. All of us can walk the path He walked when, with His words ringing in our ears, His spirit filling our hearts, and His teachings guiding our lives, we choose to follow Him as we journey through mortality. His example lights the way. Said He, "I am the way, the truth, and the life" (President Thomas S. Monson, "Ponder the Path of Thy Feet", October 2014 General Conference, with permission).

14 July 2015

NST and ultrasound went great this morning. Baby is rocking it still and even fist bumped the "screen" for us. I texted my hubby to let him know that it is officially countdown time: 24 days to go! His response: CARRRRAAAAAZZZZZY!

16 July 2015

Today would be my normal chemo day. I love getting a longer break for recovery as I get closer to delivery, and I'm feeling great. Right now I'm at the doctor's, getting my NST and reflecting on how far I've come. I'm halfway through chemo, for real this time!

The first couple chemos were the easiest, but each one brings something extra to the table. There are many possible side effects that I have, thankfully, never experienced. I thought I would make a list of what I have experienced (caused by chemotherapy) for the record. Not all of these things were at once, so don't think this all just hit me one day and never went away. I think I've had it pretty easy compared to what I might have experienced. I am grateful that my body seems to handle all this trauma so well.

Chemo drug (5 treatments down) - Adriamycin and Cytoxan, aka 'Red Devil':

- Hair loss—check
- red urine—check
- fatigue/exhaustion – check
- hemorrhoids—check
- yeast infections – check
- anemia—check (still in normal pregnancy range)
- dry mouth-check
- sensitive gums and teeth—check
- strange discolored and curved nails—check
- neuropathy—check.

What I am SO glad that I haven't experienced: nausea/vomiting, mouth sores, or heart failure—obviously. One more Red Devil to go, and then it will be baby time and on to the next chemo: Taxotere.

20 July 2015

Last Red Devil!!! Last chemo while pregnant!! YAY!!! Today I'm testing out my new, homemade ice gloves. Icing hands and feet during infusion helps decrease the chance of long-term peripheral neuropathy. I'm getting some funny looks, but I don't care. Ice gloves will be my miracle makers.

21 July 2015

Day after chemo #6 is going well. I'm just really tired. I had my Neulasta shot this morning and my back is starting to hurt a bit earlier than usual, but it isn't too bad. My mom is back from being gone for a couple of weeks to attend

my family's reunion. My sister and her kids came to visit and help out last week and they are leaving tomorrow. We've had fun together and the boys have loved having cousins to play with. One good day, we even ventured out to our local Farm Country with all the kids. I really don't know how people can do chemo with young kids without lots of help. I have been blessed.

This afternoon, I'll head to my OB/GYN's office for an NST, ultrasound, and visit with the doc. So far so good. I can't believe baby will be here in two and a half weeks! Time to take my chemo stuff out of my travel bag and replace it with hospital/baby stuff for delivery. It's nice having such a wonderful distraction to keep my mind focused on family and our new addition.

22 July 2015

Third day after chemo #6 is going well. My back is still sore, but I'm sure being hugely pregnant is exaggerating it. I am SO happy to say that I think the ice gloves during infusion have been working for my neuropathy. The gloves are made from fabric sewn into what looks like big oven mitts, with pockets on both sides for two ice packs per hand and foot. I just have a minor amount of tingles after this last chemo. I also added a Vitamin B12 supplement to my daily pill regime to help with my nervous system.

While my sister was here I let her paint my toenails. They look so pretty. Feeling like a woman again is refreshing. I didn't have her do my fingernails, because I wanted to be able to keep an eye on them. I can see lines on all of my nails. These lines are called Muehrcke's nails. They are often a sign of an underlying health problem, or in my case of cancer. They are like white tree rings appearing on my nails each time I have chemo and my system goes into shock. They are actually kind of cool looking. My two thumbnails are becoming slightly discolored to brown/black. I've been putting Tea Tree oil on them every day in hopes that I won't lose them. Nail loss is a common side effect of chemo, so it won't be a shock if they do bite the dust.

I am so excited for baby to get here; it's really helping with my motivation to get better faster. A countdown chain has been made and we're all excited to meet our miracle baby. Oh, today is my oldest son's first day of cub scouts! I feel like I'm supposed to be an adult now that I have a boy this old, or does having a boy in scouts magically make me an adult? He is so excited.

24 July 2015

35 weeks gestation today! Time has really flown by. To be honest, when I first found out I had cancer, I envisioned myself in a horror movie, with cheeks sunken in, looking sick-near-to-death with my protruding belly and with baby scratching its way out. I was sure that's how it would be. I'm so glad I'm doing well. Chemo hasn't been fun. I obviously wish I didn't have cancer, but my Father in Heaven has been kind. Treatments have run smoothly with no hospital stays yet. My next goal is to not go into early labor in the next five days to give my immune system a chance to recover. Going into labor while my immune system is at its weakest worries me.

28 July 2015

Strep throat + sinus infection + four doctor's appointments today. Just keep swimming. Just keep swimming. Baby will be here in ten days!

1 August 2015

Today was a beautiful day. My oldest son has chosen to follow the example of Jesus Christ by being baptized and receiving the gift of the Holy Ghost. I am proud of him for initiating inquisitive conversations over the past several months as we have studied the Book of Mormon and the gospel. We

A full term belly, an itchy wig, and a perfect day

were so glad to have family here to celebrate with him and so many friends to support him in his decision. I even pulled my wig out to blend in.

3 August 2015

Last night I slept for five hours straight! I feel like a new woman. No waking up to my usual post-chemo cotton ball mouth, no ear pressure, no sore throat, which means my immune system is back and I'm feeling good. We had an amazing weekend with family visiting for my son's baptism. This is going to be a fun and busy week as we prepare for baby day on Friday!

4 August 2015

Our countdown chain says only three days left before another little man joins our crazy crew. We can't wait to meet him!

6 August 2015

A big batch of freezer meals were delivered to our home today. Adding these to the gifts, cards, calls, and encouragement over the past weeks/months has me reflecting. I am amazed at the generosity of others. Our service angels inspire me to be a better person. I wish I could individually thank each person to the extent that they deserve, but for now this will have to do.

As we went through the meals, organizing them to put in the freezer, my mom started to cry. My six-year-old asked why she was crying. I told him that sometimes our heart fills up with so much love and gratitude that there just isn't enough room, so the happiness leaks out of our eyes.

Our hearts are definitely full. Thank you! Thank you! Thank you! I have had four C-sections and each one has terrified me. In the weeks leading up to delivery, I have had recurring nightmares of lying naked in a cold operating room, being cut open by half a dozen masked people. It has caused me anxiety and quite a bit of worry in the past. I can truly say that I know my Father in Heaven has heard the many prayers in our behalf and has shown me great mercy.

I am not afraid. I am calm. I'm having a baby tomorrow, and he will be beautiful. I am filled with excitement and joy that tomorrow I get to meet our fifth mini man!

Chapter Five

-The New Start-

7 August 2015

We arrived at the hospital at 5:15 a.m. The sky was dark, and we were wide awake. Surgery preparations took about an hour and then I was wheeled into the operating room. Brett got his surgery room guest monkey suit on and came prepared with the camera and entertaining discussion topics to distract me during the surgery. Without hair to insulate my head, I was shivering. I was glad that I had packed my winter hat so I wouldn't freeze in the OR. The nurses, doctors, and staff were all friendly and fun to chat with. It is bewildering how by my fifth C-section I can laugh and talk with strangers as I awkwardly succumb to anesthesia, mostly naked, in a bright room.

The pre-surgery preparations and delivery went smoothly. In fact, this was by far my best and "easiest" C-section. The usual groans and motorboat noises that escape my mouth as they apply ridiculous amounts of pressure to my abdomen actually came out in the form of loud laughter this time around. With my other boys, the hardest emotional part of delivery day was right after their births. They would place the small, newly delivered body only on my shoulder for a brief introduction just before baby and dad leave for tests, cleaning, and monitoring.

When all the excitement of delivery was gone, I felt empty. Emptiness from having a baby inside me for so many months, only to be removed from my body, then removed from my sight, and leaving me in the cold OR alone with masked strangers. I would then be wheeled off to be monitored in another room, alone. Anywhere from two to eight hours would pass before I was able to hold my babies again. I did not know any different, but it was hard.

Today was different and full of miracles.

The doctors and nurses allowed skin-on-skin time right after his birth, and my sweet baby stayed with me for nearly the entire day. To have him lying on my chest, as they completed the surgery, and for those first hours after, was the greatest blessing and tender mercy to be given for the last delivery of my life.

I felt the baby's warm, fast breaths on my skin and heard his first little whimpers. He is beautiful. He is perfect. I am beyond grateful and amazed at the love my Father in Heaven offers me. I feel honored to be a mother welcoming this fifth baby boy into our lives. He saved my life and I saved his; we will forever hold this special bond.

From his beginning, he has been a warrior and a survivor. We could think of no more fitting name than Brett Garnett Partridge, Jr., after his dad. I learned that Garnett means "armed with a spear" which is a fitting name for this warrior boy who managed to make it through six rounds of chemotherapy healthy, strong, and with more hair than me.

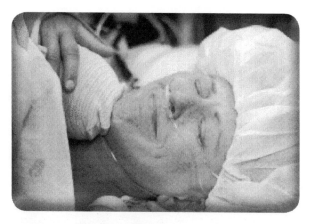

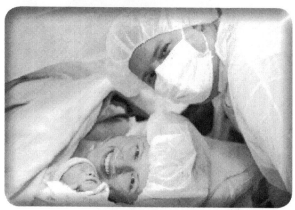

Chapter Six

-The Short Break-

Our miracle baby slept in a drawer. He will probably think that's really funny when he's older. With my mom staying in the would-be nursery, we thought that having Brett Jr. in a small bed in our room would be best. We knew the sleeping situation would be temporary, so we tried to make do with what we already had. I must say that his drawer was pretty dang cute and cozy. I sewed a cover on a fitted cushion that slid perfectly into the bottom of the drawer and he snuggled onto it for afternoon naps, nighttime, and tummy time during the day. His older brothers were envious of the drawer and often tried to sit or lie on it when he wasn't there.

I began to feel like we lived in a parallel world; enjoying our newborn while fighting for the longevity of my own life. Thirteen days of mothering passed quickly before reality called me back to chemotherapy. I clung to those thirteen days of his warm new body against my sick broken one. I wanted time to stop in those thirteen days of wrapping his tight, skinny fingers around one of mine. He was so small, so vulnerable. He depended wholly on me to feed him, hold him, and love him. It would be too soon before I would again have to depend on others to care for both of us. In a way, I felt like we were in the same place. I had so looked forward to holding him. I hadn't internalized that I still had more treatments to go. I didn't want to have to worry about chemo or surgeries. My motivation to continue with treatments was gone.

I recall a vacation Brett and I went on several years ago with our family. We enjoyed a beautiful, warm beach and learning how to surf. The water was clear, and the waves were small and perfect for beginners. Brett really caught on to surfing and was having a blast. I had fun in the water, but whenever I got onto my board I drifted straight toward a rocky area coming off the shore. Then I would have to jump off my board before I crashed. Each time the same thing would happen, and I was frustrated that everyone else seemed to surf straight to the sandy beach.

The surfing session was nearly concluded when someone yelled to me, "Stop looking at the rocks! When you get on the board, look at the beach!" This solution seemed too easy. I got on my board and kept my eyes on the sandy beach in front of me, and that's where the surfboard took me! The dangerous rocks were still there, but this time, by focusing on the beach I surfed straight to my desired destination.

I could see how my current situation required the same words of wisdom. I needed to really ponder on what I wanted my "destination" to be. Throughout my treatments, my goal had been to bring this healthy baby into the world. He was my guiding motivation. I wanted to stay positive during each chemo treatment for the baby. Now that he had arrived, the incentive was gone. I just wanted to pretend it was a bad dream and be a mom again. Once again, I found myself falling into depressive, hopeless thoughts: "Will this ever end? I'm being robbed of my newborn!"

Brett and I both expressed to each other our desire to throw in the towel and leave the thought of cancer behind us. We were physically and emotionally exhausted. With this new, beautiful, perfect baby in our arms, we wanted nothing more than to have things back to normal. The kids fighting, the fingerprints on the windows, the syrup spilled on the table – all of the messy, tiring, crazy life of parenting young children was all we wanted, no more cancer. So we had to refocus. With a perfectly imperfect picture in our minds of our children driving us crazy in the future, we knew we needed to hang on a bit longer. My new "safe shore" was a lifetime of memories with my house full of boys.

I went swinging on the swing set at the school playground with my two older boys during a "meet the teacher" night. We tried to see who could get the highest. I loved reaching my toes out so that it looked like I was kicking the clouds away in the sky and feeling the breeze flowing through my hat, even though I started feeling queasy after a few minutes. I jumped in puddles with my toddler, and I didn't care how muddy we got. I will treasure all of these little moments more than I ever had before. I am so grateful for my change in focus.

Cancer can do a lot of damage, but it cannot take away my faith in God, my laugh, my love, or my will. Surrounding myself with positive people and a supportive husband helped me refocus away from the "rocks" in this process and toward the smooth sandy shore.

Life can be really hard sometimes, but that doesn't have to change who we are at the core. We are children of God, and He has a plan for us that is pretty amazing. When we remember not just who we are, but *whose* we are, we can walk taller, care less about "stuff," and care more about preparing ourselves for everything God intends us to be. He makes big plans, and every single person that allows themselves to be led (and sometimes carried) by Him has the opportunity to see things as they really are: trials are temporary, pain doesn't last forever, and setbacks are only opportunities to do it a better way. One of my favorite quotes of all times best iterates my feelings:

> "No pain that we suffer, no trial that we experience is wasted. It ministers to our education, to the development of such qualities as patience, faith, fortitude and humility. All that we suffer and all that we endure, especially when we endure it patiently, builds up our characters, purifies our hearts, expands our souls, and makes us more tender and charitable, more worthy to be called the children of God... and it is through sorrow and suffering, toil and tribulation, that we gain the education that we come here to acquire and which will make us more like our Father and Mother in Heaven" (Orson F. Whitney quoted by Spencer W. Kimball in Faith Precedes the Miracle, 1972, p. 98, with permission).

13 August 2015

Yesterday I lost three more eyebrow hairs and two eyelashes. It never used to phase me when I lost a hair, but now that I can easily count my eyelashes on each eye in single digits, suddenly the loss of one becomes an occasion. I'll be starting my new chemo cocktail one week from today.

My stomach has butterflies already as I again approach the ever-unknown reactions to the next chemo beast. I did some research last night on my new chemo to help prepare myself and stock up on recommended supplements and helps. I was this nervous and had the same fears when I started the Red Devil, and that was doable. Now that it's finished I feel fine.

I hope and pray that my reactions will be similar with this new concoction. For now, I'll do my best to focus on preparing the kids for the upcoming school year and loving my sweet miracle baby.

I have been sprouting short blonde fuzz on my head. It will fall out again as soon as I start up chemo again, but seeing a new color is kind of fun. I wonder what it will look like when it does come back for real. I think sprouting some chia-head fuzz will be my Christmas wish this year.

16 August 2015

Today I attended all three hours of church. I can't remember the last time I was able to make it through all three hours. I've either been too sick or my immune system is too low, so I haven't felt safe around crowds of people for too long. My mom stayed home with the baby and toddler so I could do this.

It was incredible. Within a few minutes of sitting down I listened to the piano playing hymns as people found their seats and I started to cry. My inner voice kept yelling: "Stop crying! Stop crying! It hasn't even started!" Luckily, I was able to minimize the tears by focusing on keeping the kids somewhat reverent. The boys were uncharacteristically well behaved. They all wanted to sit RIGHT next to me the whole time, and I didn't mind at all.

They miss having me with them at church. Despite their misbehaving, outside-voice- projecting, and bickering during sacrament meeting, I really miss being with them too.

I've taken for granted the added spirit of the Lord that going to sacrament meeting brings to our family. I may not always hear the people speaking (that's actually more like, "I *rarely* hear the people speaking") or sing the hymns being sung. I've spent many sacrament meetings wrestling down runaway children, catching toys being flung from our pew, and attempting to calm a fussy child needing a nap. In spite of all of this, somehow the Lord has always blessed us for trying and for just showing up.

I felt those blessings today. I heard very little of the talks, but I felt the comforting peace of the Spirit of the Lord. It was not because of my attention to the speaker but because I was there. I don't know how fast my recovery will be after my next chemo, but I hope I will be able to attend all of church again soon. The Lord blesses us for our efforts, even when we fail to do it "right."

I am grateful for those who talked to me, gave me a hug, or offered a smile. I am edified and strengthened just by their presence. Today I went on a walk, I went to church, and I had a pillow/tickle fight with my boys without feeling tired by the end of the day. Miracle Baby is doing great too. He's sweet and snuggly and has been sleeping four hour stretches at night. Tender mercies.

18 August 2015

We went up the canyon near our home to make s'mores in the woods for a fun family activity. Being in the mountains is one of our favorite outings and family normalcy makes everything easier. The kids got dirty. We walked around enjoying God's creations and feeling the peace of nature. It was like our family was back to how it should be. The stickiness of the melted marshmallows and the chocolate smeared on all the boys' faces and hands brought me so much joy. I love their youth, their excitement at life, their innocence and purity. My mother heart is full today.

19 August 2015

Chemo returns tomorrow. A whole month off chemo has really made a difference in my energy level and overall well-being. I'm not looking forward to starting the craziness again, but I am looking forward to getting it done and over with so I can enjoy my baby more. There are only four "hard" chemos left and then I'll have the mastectomy, radiation, and reconstructive surgery.

My new chemo is a cocktail of Herceptin (which I will have every three weeks for the next year), Perjeta (increases effectiveness of other drugs), and Taxotere (the beast). In preparation for the new chemo, I've done research and have a new supplement plan. I'm sure more will be added to this list once I've figured out how my body reacts to Taxotere, but here's what I have placed in my old lady pill box: Supplement Roll Call:

- Vitamin d3
- Frankincense
- DDR Prime: cellular complex
- Turmeric Curcumin
- Fish Oil: healthy heart
- B-12: nervous system, energy
- probiotic: gut health
- Veggie capsule: overall health
- Fruit capsule: overall health
- L-glutamine: joint pain, faster recovery

I also will be taking other supplements to combat side effects, once they occur. Everything I take has been approved by my oncologist. I believe in both modern AND holistic approaches to healing.

20 August 2015

Chemo day is going well so far. We got to the cancer center at 9 a.m. We were warned that my new chemo would be a long one, so we came prepared with three bags, the baby and car seat, and a partridge in a pear tree. It looks like we're ready for a long weekend trip.

It's 2 p.m., and I have completed my pre-chemo drugs (steroids, anti-nausea, Benadryl), Perjeta, and I am currently halfway through the Herceptin bag. They'll finish off the infusion with the Taxotere. Benadryl totally knocked me out, so I napped for a while. One of my chemo buddies was here, so that was nice having another "sister" to chat with until I started slurring my speech and finally dozed off.

Drugs do funny things. Brett took the baby back home  when I started getting drug loopy. I'm so glad he can be here with me. His support makes me less anxious and calms my nerves.

We left the cancer center at 3:30 p.m. So far I'm reacting better to this chemo than the Red Devil, at least for day one. I fell asleep this evening, and was feeling nauseated but not too bad. Yay!

21 August 2015

I've concluded that Taxotere is my favorite (if you can have a favorite poison), at least so far. Last night I even went on a short walk to the end of our street and today I went on a longer walk around our block. I'm really feeling well. The only side effects I've felt so far is some minor nausea, a few hot flashes, and a bit of back pain.

I'm prepping myself for a crash at some point, because some people say they experience their crash a few days after treatment. For now, I'm loving the energy and being able to do normal tasks.

Here's a funny story: My husband confessed to me today that he was tempted to pick off my last few eyelashes when I fell asleep at infusion yesterday. He says it's like a comb over, and I should just let them go. Hahaha! I think he's pretty funny, and I am totally hanging on to my comb over eyelashes and eyebrows!

23 August 2015

Cancer is scary. Chemo is scary. But, who says being scary means we have to fear it? There are a LOT of things in this world that are really scary. We have a choice: allow ourselves to be paralyzed and debilitated by our fear or continue to live our lives knowing that this is just a small speck of time in God's plan for our eternal progression.

So, instead of "why me?" thinking, where we are led by fear of the unknown, we can change our life expectations to "what does God want me to learn from this?" It is the difference between mortal fear and Godly fear. Mortal fear is all of those "insignificant" things that cut into our vision of how our life should be (loss, sickness, debt, disasters, failed relationships, etc.). Godly fear is loving and trusting in our Eternal Father in Heaven, who is also an all-powerful God, who loves us and wants us to reach our highest potential and happiness.

I sometimes allow myself to be consumed by needless fear. It doesn't take too long before I realize that I need to look to Christ and press forward with faith. As soon as I allow Christ into my heart and mind, my fears shrink and I feel love and joy.

We, as a family, are so grateful and blessed to have such a large number of people supporting us and cheering us on. Surrounding ourselves with loving, kind people has really helped us keep that Godly perspective on life.

Through people's service and generosity, we are reminded how much our Father in Heaven cares for each of His children. I am thankful for the support groups that I am a part of. I am thankful to the organizations and charities that are here to lighten my load. I am especially thankful to my hubby for staying level headed and being my strength when I forget God's plan for me. I am grateful for the months that my mom has stayed with us through treatments. Now that the baby is born, and the new chemo seems more manageable, she will be heading back home to be with my dad over Labor Day weekend. Life is good, and we are grateful.My back is sore and I have dry mouth among a few other things, but I am alive.

25 August 2015

Taxotere is still my favorite, but the drugs are definitely starting to run their course. I wanted to record my Taxotere side effects so far. I read that a lot of people didn't experience side effects from this chemo until days after, so I was prepared for that. It was great coming home from chemo feeling well, having a relaxed but productive weekend, and going to church. On Monday, I started to feel my back pain increase and nausea settling in more. Today I have the works: back pain, sore/sensitive gums, nausea, diarrhea, blurred/spotty vision (luckily only for about an hour today), hemorrhoids, dry mouth, and a sore throat. I think the worst of it is the back pain and nausea; other side effects are just annoyances.

I upped my dosage of the L-Glutamine (still within recommended dosage), and I think that's helping. As long as I stay on the clock with the Zofran, nausea is manageable. I was able to do homework with the kids, go to a doctor's appointment, and take a walk with one of my boys tonight. I see mobility as a successful day. Now that I know what to expect, I'm sure I can manage my meds and supplements better after my next chemo before the side effects hit.

Also, after soaking in an Epsom salt bath for an hour and rubbing Deep Blue lotion on my back and Digestzen on my stomach, I'm feeling pretty dang awesome at the moment.

29 August 2015

Do not attempt to draw in eyebrows when you have none, they look weird. No, I will not show you picture evidence, but I will be making appearances at your local circus. Applying fake eyelashes can also prove to be pretty complicated without the eyelash guide of the originals, but they are more doable.

As an update, I'm feeling GREAT! My back pain went away yesterday and I'm hoping I'm at the tail end of my nausea. Today is all about getting work done and having fun with my family.

2 September 2015

It never ceases to amaze me how kind and genuinely concerned people are for me and my family. I think that some people think I'm lying when I say I'm doing well, but it's the truth. I'm not allowing cancer to rule my life or my mind. When I'm feeling great, I really do feel completely normal. It is not all the time, but I'll enjoy it when I have it.

If it weren't for those dang mirrors reminding me that I am pale and missing a lot of hair, I might forget that I'm supposed to be sick and cancer-y, if that even makes sense. I haven't had any nausea since last Saturday, and the back pain was pretty bad but it only lasted three days. Taxotere also causes hair loss and nail damage, but for now I have nice, soft peach fuzz on my head. I don't want to get my hopes up too high because there's still a good chance it will fall out again after my next chemo. Seeing this little fuzz is refreshing to know that I haven't lost my ability to grow hair.

I had to get something at the mall tonight. The girl at the cashier desk had this incredibly thick, long, perfectly wavy hair. She complimented my hat and I thanked her and informed her that it was a cancer patient hat. I quickly flashed her my slightly fuzzy, baldish head. Her response: "Wow, I really wish I could pull that off. I don't think I could do no hair." She made me smile. I don't think many women opt for baldness, but good for her for trying to think of a response. It's okay if you don't know what to say in an awkward situation, but I kind of love it when people say weird things anyway.

8 September 2015

I have a notebook that I've been using to record when someone does something for us during my cancer treatments. The list is not short. There have been one hundred or more hours of service that we have been the recipients of: watching kids, making meals, mowing our lawn, sending notes, bringing activities for the kids to do, not to mention a myriad other thoughtful gestures. That, along with the months my mom has stayed with us doing dishes, laundry, and watching kids when I have been at appointments. My notebook and my heart are filled.

I know some people fight cancer alone, and my heart hurts for them. Some of the greatest battles a person fights with cancer (or any trial) are mental and spiritual. That is a fight that is greatly fortified through support, faith, prayers, and love of others. We have been blessed to have that support.

I know getting through this pregnancy and chemo would have been very difficult if it weren't for my mom staying with us, my husband's constant support and presence during each treatment, and the dozens of others who made all of this easier on us.

I wanted to thank you who already have and are serving us. You have taught me how to be more charitable. You have taught me gratitude. You have taught me what it means to depend on the Lord and have greater trust in His Atonement. I hope someday to repay someone else the kindness you have shown me.

10 September 2015

Eight chemos down, only two left! The infusion went well today, and an hour was cut off the infusion time because they didn't have to give me Benadryl. I talked to my Doc about my hair growth and he reminded me not to get too attached to it because Taxotere is more potent for hair loss than the Red Devil, but I'll enjoy it while I have my soft fuzz. I can still hope that it will stay. I also asked about my specific cancer stats again, because I was getting nervous about information I had read online.

According to a prominent women's cancer charity organization, one in three cancers in women diagnosed with early stage breast cancer will metastasize (spread to other parts of the body). He checked my file for a couple of minutes and corrected my online scare by telling me that my aggressive cancer has worse numbers: 77% chance of metastasizing. Oh, great. BUT those stats are if they are left untreated.

Once I have finished chemo, mastectomy, and radiation, my numbers look much better at only a one in six chance of reoccurrence. Hearing good news is a treat to my ears. Once again, I am grateful that I caught my lump early and have been able to get through these treatments so well.

11 September 2015

Last night, I went to my first Lifting Hearts Breast Cancer support group meeting. I was only able to make it for part of the meeting, but it was great to surround myself with people that can understand and give advice. No matter what your trial, you are never alone and it is refreshing to be reminded that there is good company everywhere.

While I was reading through the papers I received last night at the meeting, I picked out these fun tidbits: "Don't ever open an oven door with a wig on or you will melt your bangs!" Hahaha, I hadn't thought of that! "Without enough sleep, we all become tall two-year-olds." So true!

14 September 2015

Taxotere is known to mess with taste buds. I think it's starting. Hmmm, I wonder what kinds of unique foods I can eat once everything taste like metal? Maybe I'll begin with trying sushi or something equally awful (sorry sushi-loving friends). Right now, I'm loving not having crazy fatigue. I'm managing my back pain well this time around, so that's making life a lot easier too. I'm also finding so much gratitude and love for my five cute boys.

15 September 2015

I planted two medicinal aloe plants shortly after being diagnosed so I could have pure aloe for radiation treatments. I read an article about transplanting and harvesting aloe. The article said that you have to remove the baby plants from the mother plant, or the new growths will basically devour the mother plant. There's a comical object lesson to use one day with that information. Wow, being a parent is hard sometimes, even for plants. Babies grow up so fast.

17 September 2015

Yesterday when Brett got home from work, I told him that my jeans were feeling loose and getting baggy around the waist. Was I losing weight? Nope, somehow I had forgotten to zip and button my pants. Oops! I can't decide if I should blame that on chemo brain or menopause brain. With either one, the odds are not in my favor.

25 September 2015

Baby's hair and my hair almost match in length! I have a good amount of growth on my head and the sprouting hair is much lighter than my natural color. It's kind of a dirty blond/brown. I also see quite a bit of gray, but it might just be ashy blonde. Yeah, let's go with ashy blonde.

The emerging hair is not pokey at all, like I expected. The fuzz is growing in very soft and fine, just like Baby's hair. AND I put mascara on today! Not long ago, I had three eyelashes left, just barely hanging on. My eyelashes now are short and stubby, but there are a lot and that makes me happy.

27 September 2015

During a class at church, we spent the time talking about the infinite Atonement of Jesus Christ and His glorious Grace. In closing the meeting, we sang "How Great Thou Art." The woman playing the piano apologetically told us that she only knew how to play the top hand to the song. As we started to sing I could hear a variation of voices and musical abilities of women from all walks of life. Some voices were loud, and some were barely audible. Not all the voices were in tune, and some were worthy of performance. I could hear the piano softly playing in the background and I was filled with awe for my Savior.

The goal of the musical number was not to sound perfect. The goal was to welcome the Spirit into our hearts and praise the Lord for His goodness and mercy. The whole lesson was summed up in this one hymn. We are not perfect. We are not worthy of God's presence just as we are, but we show up anyway. We do the best we can anyway. However slow and inept we come, we follow the Savior anyway. Despite all of our inadequacies and imperfections, He opens His arms and lovingly welcomes us in. This is grace. This is mercy. This is the love of our perfect and loving God who hears and sees our weaknesses and loves us anyway. Then in turn, rewards us with more than we deserve or could conceive on our own. How Great Thou Art!

28 September 2015

On Monday nights we gather together in our living room as a family and sing, pray, and share a lesson and scripture together followed by some kind of family activity. We each take turns being in charge of the different parts of Family Night. Tonight, our oldest (eight-years-old) was in charge of sharing a scripture. He wanted to tell us the story of Jonah. It went like this (although this is abbreviated):

"Jonah was told by God that he needed to go to a faraway land where they slapped each other with fish all the time. He didn't want to go, so he got on a ship of pirates. They played cards. Then he got eaten by a giant whale. Three days later the whale pooped him out. Then he went to 'Minima' and told them to stop hitting each other with fish. . ."

My new goal is to read the story of Jonah from the Bible to my boys. I may have them watch less Veggie Tales too. My four-year-old chose to get out Halloween stuff for the activity. They tried all the costumes on and it was a fun night.

It is almost October. I feel it is only fair to let everyone know that not all breast cancer fighters and survivors love the pink ribbon and all the hype in October. When it comes to people with breast cancer, there seems to be two camps: those who embrace the pink and those who absolutely resent it. I'm in the pink camp, but I understand the anti-Pinktobers. Here's the thing: October has become a multi-million-dollar campaign embraced by many companies and businesses. Yet, little to no money from those purchases go toward research, lowering cost of treatments, or finding a cure.

Many people dislike that breast cancer is often given a pretty face with pink ribbons, teddy-bears, and girly t-shirts boasting funny phrases about boobies. Breast cancer is anything but cute or pretty; it is ugly, painful, and destructive. I like to think of the "pink" as a bright hope in a tunnel of uncertainty. Not all stories end badly. But, I can see why some people don't like their suffering paraded around in pink rhinestones. Just think before you pink.

29 September 2015

I started feeling tingles and sensitivity to my scalp a few days ago but was hoping it would pass. I guess I can add losing my hair TWICE to my adventure list this year. Farewell, my fuzzy hair friends. It was good to see you again.

5 October 2015

I had another chemo on the first of October and did pretty well for a few days. I'm not having a great day today, but it is better this afternoon than it was this morning. I had crazy equilibrium issues when I woke up. I kept running into walls and walking sideways, but it started improving around noon. I'm feeling a lot more balanced now, but I for sure won't be going to the gym tonight.

6 October 2015

Here's a quick shout out to my frozen grape friends. During my Red Devil and Taxotere infusions I always chewed on frozen grapes. They make my mouth completely numb, slowing blood flow to that area. The reduced blood flow decreases the odds of getting mouth sores (a common side effect of both chemos). Well, I was being lazy and didn't freeze grapes for my last infusion. This morning I woke up with mouth sores. It feels like I burned my tongue. My taste buds feel scorched and sensitive. I'm sure it will go away in a few days. Yay for having the frozen grapes theory validated!

22 October 2015

10…9…8…7…6…5…4…3…2…1 and DONE! Fulfilling my treatments has taken a long six months. I was so nervous about my first chemo that I got sick to my stomach. I was terrified! It ended up being not too bad. Of all the side effects I could have gotten, I was happy with the relatively minimal issues that I had. While having my six pregnancy chemos, I experienced extreme fatigue, chronic hemorrhoids, and yeast infections, one sinus infection with strep throat, and bone pain. My last four post-delivery chemos have been much easier, with the hardest side effect being bone and back pain.

Did you know that when you are having chemo you're supposed to always have a thermometer handy? If my temperature ever reached 101 degrees I was supposed to go straight to the hospital! I got close a few times. I am glad that I've never had to be hospitalized.

People often ask how I do it and the answer is simple: lots and lots of help and love. I have had help, prayers, and service from hundreds of people. The greatest support in all of this has been Brett, the love of my life, who has been my strength and reason in chaos. To all those who have offered a helping hand or a prayer I want to say, THANK YOU! Today didn't go exactly as planned, but after shaving my head, some lab work and an EKG, I got started on my last hard chemo. Woohoo!

CHAPTER SEVEN

-The Little Things-

On October 24, I celebrated completing my last loads of toxic laundry. Twenty-four to forty-eight hours after each chemo, I had to wash all of my sheets, towels, and underclothing to discard possible chemo pollutants that I sweat out. I hated doing my "chemo-laundry," because it was another reminder of the poison running through my veins and just how toxic I was. That last load to go through the washer and dryer was done with a heart of gratitude. After recovering from the last chemo, I could stop and enjoy life, family, and the world around me with a renewed energy.

November was cold and crisp, promising snow to cover the earth. I love fall: the colors, the skies, and the sounds of crunching leaves under my feet. We walked outside as a family after school. One of my boys stomped on a pile of leaves with a big smile, proud to tell me that he was making my favorite noise. I love that crunching sound. I was grateful and filled with joy each day, knowing that I felt alive and knowing that feeling would continue. There would be no more poison running through my veins. All of the insignificant things that I missed were overwhelmingly beautiful. Every little thing.

The trees in fall are most beautiful just before they lose all their colorful leaves. The deep green leaves transform into gold and crimson. If trees have feelings as people do, I can only imagine the anguish a new tree must feel during the first winter months. It is cold and dark with no birds to sing or climb on its branches. Life slows for the tree and the known world to that tree seems to be passing away. The once beautiful leaves that joyfully waved in the wind and shaded its trunk from the sun, had one by one fallen from their home. The new tree may not realize the miracle that will soon come in the spring. That tree, in its first winter, might have felt broken and scared.

Sometimes it can be hard to hang on to hope when we are stripped of assumed security and desired expectations. Watching nature in fall is a visual example and reminder that we can put our trust in our Creator and that He has a plan for us. All our experiences are for our benefit and refinement. Life is hard at times, but trials do not have to last forever. There can always be a blossoming spring after a cold stormy winter. The lyrics to "Master the Tempest is Raging" (by H.R. Palmer) bring me comfort and beautifully articulate the thoughts I wish to convey:

Master, the tempest is raging!
The billows are tossing high!
The sky is o'er shadowed with blackness.
No shelter or help is nigh.
Carest thou not that we perish?
How canst thou lie asleep
When each moment so madly is threat'ning
A grave in the angry deep?
Master, with anguish of spirit
I bow in my grief today.
The depths of my sad heart are troubled.

Oh, waken and save, I pray!
Torrents of sin and of anguish
Sweep o'er my sinking soul,
And I perish! I perish! Dear Master.
Oh, hasten and take control!
Master, the terror is over.
The elements sweetly rest.
Earth's sun in the calm lake is mirrored,
And Heaven's within my breast.
Linger, O blessed Redeemer!
Leave me alone no more,
And with joy I shall make the blest harbor
And rest on the blissful shore.
(Chorus) The winds and the waves shall obey thy will:
Peace, be still.
Whether the wrath of the storm-tossed sea
Or demons or men or whatever it be,
No waters can swallow the ship where lies
The Master of ocean and earth and skies.
They all shall sweetly obey thy will:
Peace, be still; peace, be still.
They all shall sweetly obey thy will:
Peace, peace, be still.

That cold November, when the leaves had fallen and the sunsets turned the sky a blaze of golden oranges and pinks, was my internal spring. My dormant, dark months of winter were gone and before me was hope, light, and life. Ahead of me were more surgeries, medications, and treatments, but I felt that the hardest part was finished. I felt peace in my heart. My fears were calmed. I couldn't imagine a more beautiful place than our home, surrounded by my family, with life somewhat back to how it was, back to normal.

With such young children, our goals for family night were simple. We aimed to have a prayer, a wiggle song, and a short lesson about something like how to fold our arms for prayer or why we shouldn't kick people. The evening usually ended with one or two children running away or someone crying because a brother looked at them wrong. I do not remember the details of what we were discussing on a particular fall family night marked in my memory. The boys were climbing on me. My oldest two kept switching seats, which I could tell was annoying Brett. Something about the disarray, the free-spirited willfulness of my boys, the being together – all of it just overcame me with an abundant joy to be alive. I felt blessed to be with this beautiful chaos. My joy overflowed into tears that I tried to keep hidden so the boys wouldn't think I was sad.

My sweet, yet oh-so-destructive, two-year-old went upstairs. A moment later, coming back to the family room with a sock in his hand, he snuggled up on my lap. He kept looking up at me with his big brown eyes and his long eyelashes I was so jealous of. Every time he saw a tear fall from my eyes he soaked it up quickly with that little sock in his hand. He had the sweetest look of compassion in his eyes. It was a tender moment of Christ-like love shown through a child. Our child. I was again overcome with gratitude to be there in that moment. I'll be honest in saying that I was also very grateful that he chose a clean sock.

There were so many tender moments cherished with my family. I wonder if such moments were always there, but I was too busy to see them, or appreciate them. Several years ago, our second son, as a toddler, loved to "catch" the kisses we blew to him. He would pretend to pop them in his mouth and swallow them. This became a tradition in our family. We catch and swallow every blown kiss. That fall, I blew a goodnight kiss to our preschooler, who we call O-Man, and he chewed on it for quite a long time. He explained to me that he was chewing my kisses like bubble gum. Then he blew a kiss at me and said it was peanut butter. He insisted I chew extra-long as well. I loved his innocence and his life seemingly untainted by grief or pain. I worried so much about the effect my cancer would have on the boys, but these moments assured me of their resiliency, tender nature, and the Christ-like forgiveness children seem to embody.

My life isn't what I thought it would be. I never thought I would be the mother to FIVE boys. I never thought I would marry a computer nerd. When I was young, I thought I wanted a knight in shining armor to save me from my adversaries; someone who would fight my battles courageously. Brett is not that knight, and I am grateful. Brett gives me confidence and makes me feel strong enough to fight my own battles. He must have seen more in me than I saw in myself when we first met. He has always given me confidence in my own courage. Courage I didn't know I had. During all of that time with cancer, he would tell me that I was beautiful when I felt far from any beauty. I didn't understand or agree, but I was grateful and cherished his sincerity.

During those months of chemotherapy I felt more frail spiritually, emotionally, and physically than I thought was possible. In my most vulnerable moments, I had nothing to offer but myself in the rawest, most fragile form. Brett helped me not be afraid. He lifted me, strengthened me, and loved me when I had little to give in return. He was my rock and my sanity when I felt that my sphere of existence was falling apart. In the Bible, I read about Adam and Eve and how they were naked and not ashamed. I think there were parts of myself that I never unveiled, even to myself, until cancer forced me. In every sense of the word, I was naked and vulnerable before my husband, and I was not ashamed.

He saw the worst and the best of me and did not shy away. I love that he is a part of my life and has been with me in my pain.

I didn't get what I thought I wanted in life, but I love and want what I have. My reality is so much better than what I could have constructed if I were able to follow through with my own naïve ideas and expectations. I never would have known how strong I am. Pain showed me my strength.

23 October 2015

I got to meet my radiology oncologist today to make a treatment plan. He and his nurse were so amiable. I think I already love them. The radiologist told me that because I didn't have much lymph node involvement and was having mastectomies, I could opt out of radiation. My risk level was right at ten percent. If it's over that number, they strongly urge the treatment, but if it is under ten percent, they leave it up to the patient. I managed to be right in the gray zone.

If I were seventy years old I would refuse treatment. I, however, would prefer to live beyond that twenty-year mark when the research on recurring cancer ends. I chose to move forward with radiation. The good news is I only need to do five weeks, which is only twenty-five treatments. Another thing to celebrate is that I don't start until January. I can recover from surgery and the tissue expanders (I'll explain more about that later) and enjoy my Christmas. I am so happy!

I told the doctor that January would be perfect, because I have already hit my quota for new people getting to look at my breasts this year.

6 November 2015

I was the "mystery reader" in my son's class today. After I read a story, my son wanted me to show the class my sprouting hair. The kids were shocked when I took off my hat. I told them I'm battling breast cancer right now. Immediately hands rose. Kids were so excited to tell me about someone they know who has had cancer.

Four kids told me about someone that died from cancer. One sweet boy came up to me and said that his mom had breast cancer when he was three and now she's a survivor. I used to want to shield my kids from hard things to save them from pain. I see more and more that shielding them only makes life harder. I love being open with my kids and their friends so they are not afraid.

10 November 2015

A few months ago, my four-year-old scratched his knee while riding his bike. For weeks, long after the hurt went away, he would glance down, notice the scab and suddenly all the pain would come back. He would need me to kiss it and get a new band aid. That's what a wig is for me. I don't wear it often, but some days I'll be feeling great, running errands, and playing with the kids, and then I walk by a mirror and get an emotional slap in my face.

Oh yeah, I'm sick. I have cancer. That is when having a wig is convenient, not to mention it keeps my head warm when weather gets cold. It's refreshing to look in the mirror with a wig on. Instead of feeling sick, I can confidently say, "Hey there, you hairy beast. Lookin' good."

12 November 2015

Today was my first Herceptin-only infusion day! Herceptin doesn't have any side effects and is a pretty quick infusion. I'll be doing this through my port every three weeks for a year. After my infusion, I also had my first Lupron shot... yowza! Big needle right on the bum cheek, not fun. Lupron chemically shuts down my ovaries, keeping me in menopause (or many refer to it as chemopause). Lupron reduces the production of hormones that feed the cancer. The recommendation is to take this drug for five years.

After talking with my OB/GYN and oncologist, we decided to remove my ovaries sometime early next year when I've recovered from all my other surgeries. Once my ovaries are removed, I will no longer have to get the Lupron shot. Going through menopause at thirty-three years old wasn't really in my life plan, but I've always liked trying new things. Why not menopause?

17 November 2015

Some days I feel like I should wear a safety vest. I've been poked, prodded, and cut open so many times, I feel like a construction site. A few months ago, I decided I would rather have the peace of mind and symmetry from bilateral mastectomies (removal of both breasts), as opposed to only removing my cancerous breast. Today I'm getting lab work and an X-ray done to prep for that surgery tomorrow. I've heard from other survivors that it can take time before my body feels like my own again and less like a circus show. This morning I lost a whole lot of hair again, so it will be nice to stick it to cancer tomorrow.

18 November 2015

Update: My body has been marked up for surgery. I have resistant veins, and we tried warning the nurses of that when we arrived. After forty minutes of poking attempts and me passing out twice, they finally got a good vein for my IV. That was all while using the vein finder. Is it weird that Brett and I kind of want one of those for Christmas now? Vein finders are awesome!

19 November 2015

I am now one day post bilateral mastectomy. My chest feels like I've been punched several times in the ribs while wearing a tight corset. On top of that, the boiler went out on this side of the hospital. My room has been maintaining a temperature in the mid-to-high fifties. This is pretty much the worst spa day ever. They didn't even paint my nails. I'm asking for a refund.

In all seriousness, I'm doing pretty well. It is very painful but manageable, and a technician is working on getting the heater working. Tomorrow is a new day, one day closer to recovery. I am grateful for ice packs for my chest and lots of heated blankets for the rest of my body. I will get to go home tomorrow. I look forward to my own bed in my own room with my own pillows.

22 November 2015

It's been four days since my mastectomies. Being home helps with recovery. I'm pretty sure hospital beds are made to be uncomfortable so that people don't want to overstay their welcome. The pain is not too bad compared to something more severe; I've heard breaking your femur bone is the worst pain you can endure, according to the comedian Brian Regan anyway. I am still sore, but it could have been much worse. Right now, I'm hooked up to some tubes that are pretty annoying.

I have two "grenade" drains (this is a HUGE blessing because a lot of women end up with four to six of these drains). The drains go directly under my skin collecting excess blood to avoid infection and inflammation. Every eight hours, the drain bulbs get emptied out manually, measured, and recorded on a notebook I keep in my bathroom.

The tubes can be removed once I can go twenty-four hours with 30ml or less of drainage. I also wear a fancy bag, like a fanny-pack, around my neck that has numbing pain medicine. This medicine is also tubed, directly inserted under my skin beneath my rib cage. I think it will run out by tomorrow. Brett has been instructed how to carefully pull it out. I'll be shutting my eyes for that. Right now, my pain is being managed just fine with Tylenol. We'll see how I do when the tube meds run out. If I wanted no pain, I would stick with the heavy narcotics. I would rather deal with pain with a lesser pain killer and have a clear mind, which I just don't get to enjoy on stronger drugs. I am not a masochist, but I would rather experience pain and feel the difference between one day and the next as I heal than be numb, depending on a clock for my well-being. I know taking minimal drugs is not a choice for everyone, but this is how I want to heal. Everybody reacts differently to treatments and surgeries. I have been blessed with a high pain tolerance and a strong immune system. I will always be grateful for what advantages that has given me.

The hardest part of this process is not being able to play with the kids like they just started getting used to again. My two-year-old is so unpredictable with his movements, that

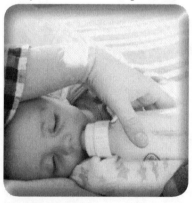 I avoid him as much as possible. I'm worried he'll playfully head-butt me or pull out my tubes. He's just too young to understand. Locking myself in my room is easier than being with him and having to constantly tell him to keep his distance.

We are grateful that my parents-in-law have been here to help out with the kids. I look forward to snuggles and wrestling in the future, but for now the boys will have to be cared for by others. There is a

noticeable improvement in how I feel each day. I think I'll be back to "normal" in a couple of weeks.

Oh I almost forgot to mention the best part; I got to shower today! Warm showers are my favorite!

24 November 2015

Surgery test results are in: CANCER FREE! I have a complete response to chemotherapy. No cancerous cells were found within the tissues tested from the surgery.

I was not anxious about my doctor appointments today. I actually forgot that they would have my pathology report from my surgery back. The peace gifted to us from our Savior's atonement is real and powerful.

Brett and I prayed in gratitude to our Father in Heaven in the parking lot of the doctor's office. We held hands and cried. This Thanksgiving will have new meaning to us. I am alive. We have five amazing boys. I have been given a new start with a new perspective and couldn't be more grateful. There are still hurdles to get past before I am finished with this whole process, but today is a day of rejoicing. "Rejoice, O my heart, and cry unto the Lord, and say: O Lord, I will praise thee forever; yea, my soul will rejoice in thee, my God, and the rock of my salvation" (2 Nephi 4:30, The Book of Mormon).

I AM CANCER FREE!

27 November 2015

To save you from what you may feel is an awkward conversation when I see you around, I thought I would give some (possibly too much) information about my mastectomies and reconstruction. A mastectomy is a total removal of the breast. I had a total mastectomy on my right side to treat my invasive ductal carcinoma. I had a prophylactic mastectomy on my left side for my own peace of mind, for prevention of future cancer, and for symmetry.

I opted to begin reconstruction during the mastectomies. The process of reconstruction is not the same as augmentation. After the entire breasts were removed, my plastic surgeon placed a tissue expander beneath my skin, which is a temporary inflatable implant. I was fully expecting to wake up from my surgery to a concave chest, but Dr. Jensen started me off with some saline already in the expander. I was relieved to wake up and see something there. Those lumps were a welcome surprise.

Every week I will go in and be injected with 100 cc's of saline, until I've reached my approximate natural breast size. I've only had one appointment so far, and I already know that injection day is painful. It took a couple of hours before it didn't feel like my ribs were being crushed and I could breathe normally. Next time I'll be better prepared and take some Aleve and Tylenol before I go.

Once I'm done with the expansion process, I will have radiation on my right side for five weeks. The radiation will damage my skin and tissue, so it will need several months to heal. Sometime in the spring, I will have my exchange surgery, where the doctors will remove the expanders and put the permanent implants in. I have two six-inch scars that run straight across my chest. They are not pretty, but it's not like they are on display anyway. (Except for the dozen or so medical professionals, of course).

As for recovery, I am doing well. I was able to pick up and carry my baby comfortably yesterday for the first time since the surgery. I have to keep reminding myself that this is a relatively short amount of time that I will have to suffer in exchange for a longer life. I still cringe when my two-year-old runs up to me, but he can now sit on my lap and softly lay on me without any pain. I probably won't be able to lift him up for another week or two.

My bruising and drains are bothering me a lot more now, which I take as a good sign, because my bigger pains are subsiding. I am doing stretches and exercises every day to help my growing muscles and tissue. It will take time before the soreness subsides. I even did some Black Friday shopping with my drains and tubes pinned under my shirt (I was worried someone might think I was shoplifting, because they bulge out under my clothing).

In summation: I did have mastectomies. Yes, I know my chest doesn't appear like I had mastectomies. Don't give me any hugs, but I take gentle high fives. Tylenol is keeping the pain at bay. Life is good.

28 November 2015

I made rolls with the help of my four-year-old. Learning to knead properly is a great life lesson and skill. Use the hardest and strongest part of your hand. Push. Turn over. Push. Turn over. The dough is not done when you're tired. The dough is done when your arms are weak and you feel your abdomen muscles hurt. Why can't we stop when we're tired? It only turns out and rises to the fluffiest rolls if we knead it until we hurt and the dough is smooth and soft. Then we know the dough is done.

30 November 2015

I've been doing the recommended post-mastectomy exercises for the past week, minus the floor stretches. I thought it would be too painful to stretch my chest that much. Today after doing three small loads of laundry, changing two beds, and getting my two-year-old down for a nap, I felt invincible. So, I lay down on the floor to do my stretches and that's as far as I got.

Yikes! I didn't think lying flat on my back would stretch me out so much. I lay there for five minutes doing nothing

and considered myself done for the day. Maybe tomorrow I'll go on my back and attempt to actually do the stretches too.

2 December 2015

I was asked if I ever felt guilty for having cancer. I've been asked this a few times, so it's probably something that more people are curious about. Short answer: Sometimes, but I try not to be.

Long answer: Shortly after being diagnosed I started asking myself the scary questions and wondering about my actions. Maybe I wouldn't have cancer if I never put my cell phone near my breast. Do I have cancer because I eat too much sugar? I try and eat healthy, but I've never been consistent about eating enough greens. Would I have cancer if I started eating healthier when I was younger?

Really, there are dozens of things that I considered and that started to scare me. I stopped eating sugar completely for a while. I bounced from Paleo, to Vegan, to whatever other diet I thought might fix it. I started only using coconut oil for cooking and got rid of our aerosol sprays. I stopped using any lotion, soap, shampoo, or anything else that wasn't made of all pure-natural ingredients. For a brief period, I just felt scared of everything.

THAT IS NOT HEALTHY!!!

Living in fear is worse than consuming a little something that might make you sick in ten years. I don't ever want to have cancer again. More importantly, I want to have a happy fulfilling life of living, not just trying not to die. I am more likely to be killed in a car accident, but that doesn't keep me from driving a car. I have made some life changes and will continue to improve my health baby steps at a time. Motivation is now less about fear and more about realizing how incredible our bodies are and wanting to care for mine as a gift from God and be healthy.

My current diet: less junk, more salads, limited red meat, more fruits, veggies, nuts, seeds, whole grains, beans, etc. I buy mostly organic when I can, but I also throw in a milkshake here and there. I want to cherish my moments and not dwell on what could have or would have been.

6 December 2015

Most of the time I am just fine, but sometimes when my back hurts, and my front hurts, and my sides hurt, and I have a cold, and my nose runs constantly because I have no nose hairs, and I still have drains, I lose my temper and I sob. Then a loving God opens His arms to me with another droplet of peace. My boys sweetly sang "I Am a Child of God" tonight and I read Philippians 4:13. "I can do all things through Christ which strengtheneth me." All is well! This is the right time to remember the baby born humbly in a stable that saved us all.

7 December 2015

It's time to meet my new little friend, my long-term prescription. I've been hanging on to this prescription for a few days. I finally took the plunge this morning and opened the bottle. The name is Tamoxifen, but I think I'll call her Moxi for short. I'll be taking one of these tiny circular pills every day for the next five years, and she packs a mean punch. This is the pill that will block hormones and keep me in menopause mode.

Side effects can be (but not limited to) hot flashes, weight gain, mood swings, and anger. I'm hoping for no side effects, but time will tell. My cancer fed off hormones, so it is important that I get rid of as many as I can to prevent recurrence. That's what this will do. Bottoms up and keep the change, ya filthy animal.

8 December 2015

I've gone cordless! Woohoo! I wouldn't have thought that the worst part of recovering from a mastectomy would be the drains, but they are SO annoying. They are itchy and make my sides sore. Taking a shower was a long process of giving myself a pep talk to get in, and then once I got in it took more pep talks to want to get out and deal with drying off. Although, I didn't mind the long showers too much. To shower I attached the drains to a lanyard that I wore around my neck. I've been wanting to get to the gym for a few weeks, but there was something about jogging on a treadmill with plastic grenades of my blood sloshing around that just kept me from going. Let me just be clear, in case you didn't get the point: I LOATHE drains!

I am SO happy to have that part of this process finished! Now I can look forward to me—cordless! I also had another "filler" today in my tissue expanders. If you've ever had a heart attack or been sat upon by an elephant you can relate. I'm now lying in bed with a nice warm hot pack rotating over my chest and then my back. The worst is the first twenty-four hours. I've never been more excited for a Wednesday. Thanks goes to my husband, who has been distracting me during the worst part of the pain by planning our ten-year anniversary, and to good friends who let my kids play at their house.

10 December 2015

The world is more beautiful today and I am happier and more patient. Why? SIX hours of uninterrupted sleep does wonders. Imagine the joy with eight!? But I won't be that greedy. I'm convinced that the leaders of the world would be more reasonable and cooperative by adding more sleep to their day and more fiber to their diets.

11 December 2015

Today I am reminded of what cancer has given me. Cancer has given me increased love, appreciation, and empathy for others in pain. Cancer has given me a view of things that are truly important and less caring about things that are not. Cancer takes, but it also gives.

12 December 2015

I love the month of December. The world seems to quiet down all the complaints and anger to be more grateful. I have a lot to be thankful for this year.

Packing is the first thing I can be grateful for right now. I love that with my limited supply of hair I don't need to account for a blow dryer, straightener, brush, and other hair products when traveling. It's absurd how much luggage space goes toward hair care products! I'm pretty much the lowest maintenance person ever now.

Another thing I am grateful for is being one week on the hormone blocking "menopause" pill and not noticing any side effects yet. I've had a few small hot flashes, but I was getting those with chemo too, so that is nothing new. If I knew last October that I was having my last ever period I would have done more to celebrate. Bring on the chocolate! Don't be too jealous, but I am pretty happy about not worrying about having a visit from Aunt Flo every time we go on a trip or go swimming. Freedom! I may be one step closer to adult diapers, but I'm okay with that.

15 December 2015

During the first two Sundays after my mastectomy, I didn't go to church because I was in a lot of pain and didn't want to be bumped. Then I got a pretty wicked cold and couldn't make it. Now I'm feeling pretty good, but two of my kids had bad coughs on Saturday night, so I ended up staying home with them. Let's hope we stop recycling this cold around our house so I can get out more. I want to be able to go to church again.

Here's how I'm doing, for those that really want to know: I'm still going in once a week to fill my tissue expanders. Many people spread this process out over several weeks/months, but I'm doing it quickly so that I can start radiation sooner. I just want to be finished with all of the cancer removing demands so I can move on, even if that means dealing with torture. Having tissue expanders filled is extremely uncomfortable and is often compared to having a heart attack. Pain is at its worst in the first few hours, but can last for a couple of days. I've heard that some people don't experience the pain as much and some only experience it for a select amount of fills. I'm hoping to get a reprieve from the pain during at least some of my fills.

On a pain scale from one (stubbed toe) to ten (the pit of despair from *Princess Bride*,) I'd give my pain a score of seven for my last fill. The first few were more like a three, but the pain has just been getting progressively more severe. I can still walk around (stiffly), have conversations, and even help kids with homework. It is hard to play with and chase my toddler and preschooler, or carry the baby just after a fill. For the first few hours I focus on breathing, because my lungs feel like they're going to collapse. Then after a couple of days I feel pretty good. I still get shooting pains in my left armpit, and I'm usually sore every morning when I wake up.

I've been told that the shooting pains will lessen over time, but will certainly feel better when I have my exchange surgery. I get really sick of being sore and in pain. Sometimes I melt down and cry, and that's when my husband tells me I should take a Tylenol or Aleve, and I do. I'm not wanting you to feel sorry for me. I'm just telling you how it is.

This is where I'm at, and I'm almost done with this part. I currently use Doterra's Deep Blue on my armpit when the scarred area is in pain. I take Aleve and Extra Strength Tylenol right before a fill and for a couple of days after. I use a hot pack almost every day. I've been told to take Percocet, but I won't. I never filled my prescription after surgery, because I hate how narcotics make me feel.

My logical self says that I have no right to complain if I'm not willing to take what's available to relieve the pain, but I don't always like to be logical. I pick pain over absolute loopiness, which is what happens to my brain on "better" pain killers. This all sounds bad, but really, I'm doing well. If you ask me how I'm doing I will answer honestly: it feels like my insides are being crushed in pain but it will ease up soon, fine, pretty good, or great. I almost always end one of those phrases with "at the moment" if I know that my status will change soon.

So, in summation, I am doing fine and will be even more fine in a few weeks when I am finished filling my expanders. I am overly excited for a short break and time to enjoy Christmas and take a vacation from my problems this week(Yes, Brett and I will be watching *What About Bob?*).

17 December 2015

I had a tissue expander fill today at my plastic surgeon's. It wasn't nearly as bad as my last one. Phew! I can't say I feel great, but pushing this fill out by two days made a difference.

My body just needs a break. My doctor and I were able to have a conversation about my options for the future and radiation treatments. When making decisions like this, it is always important to have all the information, weigh the options, and pray. Not everyone chooses reconstruction, but it was right for me. I just want to look and feel like "me" again.

20 December 2015

". . .His name shall be called Wonderful, Counselor, The mighty God, the everlasting Father, The Prince of Peace. . " (Isaiah 9:6). He is the Savior of the World, our advocate with the Father, our perfect example, and the Redeemer of mankind. In His birth, we are reminded that our Father in Heaven cares enough for us to offer His only begotten son for us. In His birth, we are reminded that God keeps His promises. Because of Him we have hope.

21 December 2015

I have the pleasure of belonging to a wonderful support group of women undergoing cancer treatments while pregnant. I've never met any of these women in person, but they are my friends, my confidantes, and my inspiration. On Saturday one of the women who started the group passed away, leaving her toddler son and husband behind.

Thinking about my friend and her family while attempting to prevent my own fears from coming back has been difficult. I love belonging to this support group, but sometimes people die in our group, and it is hard for us all.

31 December 2015

Here is a brief summary of the year:

- ✘ 46+ doctors' appointments (this does not include x-rays, blood labs, echocardiograms, etc.)
- ✘ 10 chemotherapy infusions
- ✘ 3 Herceptin infusions
- ✘ 1 lumpectomy
- ✘ 1 C-section
- ✘ 1 bilateral mastectomy
- ✘ 5 tissue expansions

Have a great night! Tomorrow is a new day and a new year and I have a good feeling it is going to be incredible.

Chapter Eight

-The New Year-

The new year came. A whole year passed since my son woke me up wanting chocolate in the middle of the night. That year felt like a lifetime, yet, there were still lots of appointments, radiation, and surgeries to be had.

Cancer treatments are like being in an astonishingly long line at an amusement park for a ride I never wanted to be on. I wait in line. Concessions sellers come by with lemonade for a brief reprieve. I wait in line. There are small spurts of celebrating when the line moves forward a few feet, but excitement fades with time. At the end of the day, I am still just waiting in a line for a ride that I never wanted to go on.

Where was my cancer fast pass? I annoyed myself with my inner voice, yelling, "Are we there yet? Are we there yet?" Years from now, I'll hopefully look back and see this as an unfortunate blip of my life's journey, like my oncologist told me months ago. At this point in treatments, however, all I could think was, "Are we there yet? Oh, and I'm ready for some more lemonade."

7 January 2016

Menopause.

The effects of menopause haven't been too bad for me, because I was going through chemo-pause during chemotherapy. I'm more educated on what it means to be a 33-year-old old lady. I've learned to dress in layers, because I never know when summer heat will join me. Forget Christmas in July - I get July in January (I know you're jealous)! I've also learned that occasional incontinence is a common occurrence in menopausal women. How I feel about that *Depends* on the day. My body is all sorts of crazy fun.

16 January 2016

I've had a few people ask about breast cancer and what comes after the "Cancer Free" pathology. First, I don't know much about other cancers. There are a LOT of different kinds of cancer out there, and I have only studied mine – triple positive invasive ductal carcinoma. There are two parts of this diagnosis that can cause some concern (other than the obvious cancer part): invasive and triple positive. Invasive breast cancer means cancer cells breached a barrier to make it outside of my cancer tumor. I was blessed to have only a small number of cells found, but there were cells found.

Triple positive breast cancer is an immensely aggressive cancer that feeds off of three different hormones in my body. Twenty years ago, this would have been a death sentence. Today, there are many treatments available for triple positive but it is still an aggressive, fast growing cancer.

Metastatic Cancer (Mets) is the only breast cancer that has a low survival rate. Some types of mets can be cured and there are many life-extending treatments. With treatments, stage four has a twenty-two percent survival rate after five years. Mets comes from an origin, or primary cancer, that has spread and invaded other organs of the body. It usually first invades the bones, brain, liver, and lungs. Even when a new tumor and cluster is formed, they still consider it breast cancer, because that was the cancer's origin.

Knowing this, you can see why many people who have had cancer become keenly aware of any and every pain, tick, or change with their bodies. Triple positive cancer that has turned into Mets is usually found within the first five years of original diagnosis. After surgery, the cancer free test result is specific to the tissue they have performed surgery on, not the whole body. This information is why survivors become hypochondriacs.

If you were completely cancer free, doctors would not require checkups every few months. When I feel slight abdominal pain, or my bones hurt, or I experience any abnormality with my body, my thoughts first go to Mets. I try to not go there, but it happens and sometimes it scares me. The absolute worst thing I can do when this happens is google my symptoms, or even worse, google my symptoms along with the word "cancer."

Internet searches = bad. I need to remind myself of this. It will be a glorious day in 2020 when I can celebrate five years cancer free and my Mets statistics drop dramatically. It's easy to see why most people with cancer can tell you how many years they have been living in remission. Each year, we celebrate that we made it one more year without a new diagnosis. Now you know.

18 January 2016

My hair is coming in more and more each week! One month ago, I had seventeen eyelashes. Now I have more than

I can count. They are short and stubby, but they're there. My eyebrows are also coming back. The eyebrows and eyelashes are the slowest to grow, but they are coming.

This is a bit random, but I find it ironic that the correct dosage for my "One–A–Day" vitamins are two vitamins.

21 January 2016

I did radiation preparation today after my Herceptin infusion. I started with a CT scan. The CT scan was kind of fun. Am I weird for closing my eyes and pretending I was driving an alien spaceship? The machine kind of sounded like a flying saucer, or at least what I assume a flying saucer would sound like. The scan was pretty relaxing.

During radiation, the machine needs to be totally precise. To prevent me from moving, they make a mold of my upper body that I lie on during the treatment. This is my own, individualized, uncomfortable, hard pillow to keep me in the exact same position every day. We made that mold just before the scan.

They also need to ensure that the radiation machine is pointed at the exact same spot every day. To do this, they put six permanent tattoo markers around the area needing to be radiated. They are small, roughly the size of a freckle. I asked the nurse (or was it the PA? I'm not even keeping track of who sees me naked nowadays.) if she could do something more than a tattoo dot on one of the markers. I'll have to get the tattoos, so why not enjoy at least one of them? Although undetectable to anyone other than my husband and doctors, I have a small inked heart just below my chest as one of the markers. I am looking forward to starting next week so that I'll be that much closer to being done.

Summary: I was drugged, scanned, and inked. Good day.

27 January 2016

Day One Radiation. As I would say to my kids, "easy peasy, lemon squeezy."

• Changed into the ever so flattering hospital gown in changing room.

• Walked through "Caution" radiation room doors while strategically holding gown shut

• Laid on the hard bed (more like a table) and found my head niche in my custom, stiff pillow.

• Held completely still with gown open and got radiated (or if you're cool, people in the cancer community call it "rads").

• Done.

The radiology nurses are awesome. They let me choose the Pandora station during treatment, so I hummed along with 80's pop the whole time. While the machine is on, the nurses are out of the room, watching and listening from a booth with monitors. The process is painless. After the treatment, I am now more aware that my shirt rubs on my skin. The chafing is not painful, just slightly more sensitive, like when you come in after being in the sun. I've already cut off my first aloe leaf to use. The burning and fatigue don't usually hit people until the second or third weeks of rads, or so I've read. One down, twenty-four to go!

January 2016

A piece of innocence and childlike naiveté was lost in my boys' eyes this last year; I lost some of mine too. In that loss of innocence, empathy has emerged. These sweet boys of ours had no qualms at offering butterfly kisses when I couldn't give them kisses in return, and accepted hand hugs instead of bear hugs when I was in pain or too weak.

Over two thousand years ago, the Son of God descended below all so that He can offer us empathy and mercy in our afflictions. While among His friends and chosen apostles, He fell asleep at sea. A storm came, and the boat was tossed about. The situation seemed dire. His apostles allowed their fears to overcome them and called to the Lord for help. Immediately, Jesus stood and commanded the storm, "Peace, be still!" There were many times this past year when I felt that I was sinking. My only comfort was to get on my knees and pray for that same peace.

Sometimes the Lord will calm the storm and sometimes He will calm the sailor, but the calm will come when I turn to Him.

1 February 2016

The radiation room is large and sterile looking. When I walk in, I see the flat, hard bed with my custom blue pillow and leg rests. They use a rubber band around my feet to keep them together. My hands hold two bars, protruding from the top of the table above my head, during treatment. The huge radiation machine moves around me, and I lie still, listening to the whirring and beeps made by the moving mechanical arm. It only takes about five minutes. The entry door is about six inches thick. I feel like I'm in a bomb shelter, only the harmful substance isn't outside; the toxins are inside the shelter with me.

8 February 2016

First was radiation, then three of my boys went to doctor's appointments for various winter illnesses. We all went to the pharmacy for ear infection antibiotics. After lunch was

Baby Bump, Cancer Lump

another doctor appointment, where my kids behaved so badly that I never want to show my face in that office again. When we got home it was time for homework, then back to the pharmacy again, followed by dinner (frozen nuggets kind of night). The kids all had an early bed time after family night, and instead of crashing on the couch I ran to the store, because we're out of milk.

Today's lineup of insane event after event has been draining. But I'm now lying in bed watching *The Office* and can't help but feel blessed. My day was crazy. My boys are crazy. Some days I want to pull the few hairs I have out because of the unruliness that is five boys eight and under. I am so happy to have that much love in my life, and I don't feel too bad about occasionally locking myself in my room for a moment of peace and chocolate during the day. The sun will come up tomorrow!

It's days like this that make me miss our puppy, Rocky. His furry, loving snuggles would be nice.

11 February 2016

One of the side effects of chemo/radiation/hormone therapy is the risk of heart failure. When testing the health of the heart they measure the ejection fraction, which is the total amount of blood in a ventricle that is pushed out with each heartbeat. A healthy person's ejection fraction is between 50-70%. I periodically have echocardiograms to make sure my heart muscle is still ticking.

Last April, my ejection fraction was at 64%. Today my ejection fraction is at 53%. I'm still in the healthy range, but the drop is not good, so they'll be monitoring it more. Cancer treatments are a bunch of weighing and balancing options. These treatments will have permanent effects on my body that I will deal with for the rest of my life. At least I'll have a life, and that's what I'll celebrate. I'm doing fine. I'm almost halfway through radiation—woohoo!

·123·

24 February 2016

Radiation burns are barely noticeable. My right breast area is darker, but my darkest radiation burns are in my armpit. I only have four more treatments. I know the skin will darken over the next week or two. To come this far without any bad burns is remarkable. My tissue on the radiated side is sore all of the time, but it is not preventing me from doing any regular activities. I can even still sleep on that side and I'm still exercising.

I have a strict skin care regimen that I have been following each day since rads began. I've been raising eight medicinal aloe vera plants since last summer, just for this occasion. The aloe stains my clothes, so I wear clothing I don't mind ruining on the days I harvest the leaves. I also use aloe gel, which doesn't stain, Miracle Skin Relief (found at a local health food store), Aquaphor, and Rescue (which was gifted to me by my radiation oncologist) every day. Rescue is my favorite. I keep it in my cold car and put it on right after treatment. It has a nice, cool, numbing sensation on my skin. I end up applying one or a combination of these, four times every day. I started doing this on day one, and I think that's the key. If you wait until you already have a burn, it will be too late.

I always go into radiation with clean/dry skin. Lotions applied before treatment will amplify the radiation and make the burns worse. I haven't gone this many days in a row showering before 8 am since I worked full time. Almost done!

27 February 2016

5:45 a.m.

4 out of 5 boys awake

2 out of 5 boys crying

The 2 out of 5 boys awake and not crying, gingerly take over our bed.

How in the world did Brett and I get such early risers?

Is it nap time yet?

29 February 2016

My 7-year-old this morning: Mom, my legs grew!

Me: You're growing all the time. Why do you say that?

Son: Because these are my new pajamas and they were longer on my legs the last time I wore them.

Me: Oh, that's probably just because I washed them, so they shrunk.

Son: (looking confused) When did you wash my legs?

1 March 2016

25 radiation treatments finished! Monday-Friday 8:30 a.m. shower, dress, burn, repeat. It really wasn't too bad for me, mostly just a time nuisance. My skin still looks pretty good except for a few inches in my armpit that are pretty fried. I kind of hate wearing shirts because it chafes my skin. I don't live in a nudist colony though, so I'll deal.

Most people complain of fatigue, which is a common side effect of radiation. I don't feel any more tired than I usually do, considering I have five boys who rarely all sleep through the night. In some ways, I feel like I have increased energy in the past couple of weeks. This is probably because I've been diligently drinking tons of water and taking veggie and fruit supplements. I'll kind of miss talking with my rads friends, Katie and Dana, who take care of me. We talk about anything, except cancer, every morning. They are so endearing. I won't miss them enough to want to go back, however.

9 March 2016

You know when you are out in the sun having fun and you realize that you might have become sunburned, but you can't really tell? The next day comes and you look in the mirror at the reflection of what appears to be a lobster with your face. Apparently, radiation works similarly. The effects don't always come until later. Most of my skin looks incredible, considering I just completed 25 radiation treatments. Those couple of inches in my armpit that I mentioned last week ended up being really burnt a day after radiation was finished. If you've ever accidentally scorched your arm on a curling iron, that's what it felt like for a few days, except it is in my armpit, which made wearing clothes awful. I rubbed silver cream, lidocaine, Aquaphor, and aloe on the burn a few times a day. Now, a week out and new skin is growing where the dead skin has peeled. My clothes no longer feel like coarse sandpaper on an open wound. Hooray for being finished with one more thing!

13 March 2016

Sometimes the answer right in front of us is the hardest to see. I can clearly see that the times in my life when I have felt the weakest spiritually have been the times that I have slacked on studying the scriptures. I came across this quote today that spoke to my heart:

> "If we don't have the word of God or don't cling to and heed the word of God, we will wander off in strange paths and be lost as individuals, as families, and as nations.... As with voices from the dust, the prophets of the Lord cry out to us on earth today: take hold of the scriptures! Cling to them, walk by them, live by them, rejoice in them, feast on them. Don't nibble. They are 'the power of God unto salvation' [Doctrine & Covenants 68:4] that lead us back to our Savior Jesus Christ.
>
> "If the Savior were among us in the flesh today, He would teach us from the scriptures as He taught when He walked upon the earth. His words ring out: 'Search the scriptures; for … they are they

which testify of me' [John 5:39]—a testimony borne by the Holy Ghost, for 'by the power of the Holy Ghost ye may know the truth of all things' [Moroni 10:5].

"What a glorious blessing! For when we want to speak to God, we pray. And when we want Him to speak to us, we search the scriptures; for His words are spoken through His prophets. He will then teach us as we listen to the promptings of the Holy Spirit" (Elder Robert D. Hales, "Holy Scriptures: The Power of God unto Our Salvation," LDS General Conference, October 2006, with permission)."

15 March 2016

I'm struggling to figure out how to best style my hair so that I don't look like a man. I feel like I have to overcompensate with makeup, but without looking like a clown. Oh, the struggles…Really, I'm not that worried. I'm just happy to have hair, and eyelashes, and eyebrows, and to be alive. Eyebrows and lashes make me feel like a woman again.

I am happy to say I don't have shingles. My doc checked out a small rash on my radiation side. I had concluded that it was either shingles or skin cancer, because I'm a hypochondriac and why not. I was SO relieved that it was actually just a small rash. Rashes are the best!

21 March 2016

Today is echocardiogram day! My first echocardiogram was done while I was pregnant just before my first surgery. It was relaxing. Something about being in a dark room while someone rubbed warm oils on my chest, with the humming sounds of my heartbeat playing lullabies made me doze off.

Post-mastectomy and tissue expander echocardiograms aren't nearly as relaxing. The tissue expander is in the way of the view of the heart, so I have to fill my lungs and hold my breath several times while the machine jabs into my rib cage. I miss the times when I used this as an opportunity to nap. I'll get the results on Thursday during my Herceptin infusion. Hopefully my ejection fraction (the percentage of blood leaving the heart each time it contracts.) hasn't declined any further.

In other news, I started wearing deodorant on my radiated side again this weekend. It has been over a month since I've been able to wear deodorant. I think my friends at the gym will thank me.

27 March 2016

> "Each of us will have our own Fridays—those days when the universe itself seems shattered and the shards of our world lie littered about us in pieces. We all will experience those broken times when it seems we can never be put together again. We will all have our Fridays. But I testify to you in the name of the One who conquered death— Sunday will come. In the darkness of our sorrow, Sunday will come. No matter our desperation, no matter our grief, Sunday will come. In this life or the next, Sunday will come" (Joseph B. Wirthlin, "Sunday Will Come," General Conference, October 2006, with permission).

30 March 2016

Happy Cancerversary!

Dear Self one year ago today,

This morning you were the mother of four rambunctious young boys, a new puppy, and an unexpected (but welcome) pregnancy, making you feel that you were at the limit of fulfillment (and stress, patience, time, and ability). After today, your view of life will be altered forever. In the coming weeks and months, you will find a depth of pain and emotional strain that you never thought was possible. You will face fear and sorrow, like never before, but you will make it through. Here are a few words of wisdom that future-you wishes you knew now:

1. Cancer will not rule your life forever. I know that right now wrapping your mind around cancer can make basic tasks debilitating. Your brain is so consumed with worry. At first, cancer penetrates every thought, action, and decision. A second may not go by without the underlying fear knocking on your brain. After some time, you'll notice that you think about it less and less. It will take several months, but I promise that it won't rule you forever.

2. The baby will be fine. I don't know how it is possible, but the chemo will not affect the baby. Trust your doctors. You will find a support group of other women just like you, pregnant with cancer. They will be your strength, your motivation, and your sustainment when you feel alone. By the way, it's a boy and he's stinkin' adorable!

3. You have to accept help and service. This will be one of the hardest parts of yourself that you will have to face. You cannot do it alone. You cannot care for your children every day. You have to swallow your pride and accept help, a lot. This year you will have to focus on getting well, which means consenting to other people's offerings and service. It will be hard to lie in bed knowing that your kids want you, but you have to rest. They will forgive you. It will not last forever. You will have good days and bad days. On the good days, you will get to be Mom. Through others' service, you will learn the true meaning of Christ-like love and charity.

4. You are the only you. Each person reacts to treatments differently. There are so many different cancers that you really can't compare your situation to anyone else's. Internet search

results will have you believe the worst of every situation. Remember, that it is more common for people to complain about bad things than to spread good news, especially in forums and reviews. You will experience some side effects but not all the possible side effects. Support groups and forums are great, but taking a break from them can be helpful too. Being supported in a community where people sometimes die can be taxing.

5. Everyone knows how to cure cancer. You will be told by dozens of people exactly what you should do to get rid of your cancer. Be grateful for their advice and warnings. They tell you these things because they love you. They will have proof. They will have real stories from people who have been healed. Along your journey, you will meet some of these people, but you will also know many people who have died using these exact same cures. Cancer doesn't abide by any one-cure-fits-all. However, your doctors have the most case studies, the most experience, and the most knowledge of what will give you your best chance. Trust them. You will find joy and feel your body strengthen as you combine holistic healing hand in hand with chemo and radiation. Cures don't have to fight each other, but people will tell you to choose one or the other. They work together well and you will be grateful for their unifying effects.

6. You will never be the same. You will want so badly to have things back to how they used to be. Your body will forever be altered. Your knowledge and understanding of life will forever be altered. Your faith in the Savior will forever be altered. You will be grateful. They call it "the new normal." When treatments are done and everything is just checkups and maintenance and the trauma is just a bad dream, you will be a different person. Your body will have a new display of scars, tattoos, aches and pains that you never had before. I know that this baby is your last, but it will be final not just by choice, but because your body will never be able to have

a child again. You will feel older. You will also feel stronger in a way that you didn't know you could. You will be more confident and less concerned over things that don't matter. You will love your husband and appreciate him more. Your new normal will be different but wonderful.

7. This is not your fault. Some people just have cancer. Some of the healthiest people will have cancer right along with the least healthy. Cancer is what you have, it is not who you are, so take it, accept it, and learn from it.

With faith and hope,
Future Stephanie

15 April 2016

There are three different kinds of cancer origins: environmental (smoking, asbestos, etc.), genetic, and sporadic. I always thought that the majority of cancers were from the first two, but in reality, most cancers are completely sporadic. Scientists believe that every person has cancer cells within their body at any given time in their life, yet most of these mutant cells don't thrive. The faulty cells should be, and usually are, filtered out by the lymphatic system and white blood cells throughout the body. I'll admit, I really didn't know anything about the lymphatic system prior to having cancer.

> "The lymphatic system is similar to the blood circulation. The lymph vessels branch through all parts of the body like the arteries and veins that carry blood. But the lymphatic system tubes are much finer and carry a colorless liquid called lymph. Lymph contains a high number of a type of white blood cells called lymphocytes that fight infection and destroy damaged or abnormal cells" ("The Lymphatic System and Cancer" web CancerResearchUK, 29 October 2014).

To decrease our chances of allowing cancer to thrive in our bodies we can remove environmental causes, be born into a new family, or give our bodies mega strong lymphatic systems. Easy, right? But seriously, aside from not smoking and avoiding licking paint with asbestos, the best thing we can do is take care of our bodies.

Keeping our bodies at a healthy weight, exercising regularly, and eating healthy gives us the greatest tools to fight infection and disease, and gives numerous other benefits to our quality of life. Eating our daily fiber and a plant based, anti-inflammatory diet is recommended to keep those white blood cells working properly. Most breast cancers are hormone driven, so be aware of any risks of hormone therapies that increase your hormone levels. An influx in hormones can actually super-charge those cancer cells. My triple positive breast cancer was dangerous during pregnancy because the added hormones in my body were just increasing the rate of growth of the cancer. As always, put thought and intention into what you allow to come into your body. Use the motto: moderation in all things. This can be applied in every aspect of living.

16 April 2016

Sometimes looking back at pictures when I was sick can bring a flow of memories of challenging times. I have changed. My miracle baby is eight months old now, healthy and happy. Who says chemo has to bring you down? This chemo charged baby is climbing on everything, crawling everywhere, and eating anything. He's a ball of joyful energy and loves his big brothers.

Chapter Nine

-The New Beginning
And The End-

I started chemo on May 7, 2015. I was terrified and sick to my stomach before treatment. Two villains, cancer and the cure, both came with their share of pitfalls, primarily death or pain. I chose life for me and life for my baby, which essentially meant choosing pain. I can imagine our spirits in the world of spirits before we came to this earth facing similar decisions. We chose to come to earth to be born into uncertainty, good and evil, and suffering, along with unimaginable joy. We chose to reject Satan and follow a plan that left us vulnerable to sin and the evil one's temptations, but also gave us an opportunity to rise above and prove to ourselves that we can and will choose [2]"the harder right over the easier wrong."

---

2   Read more about choices in "Choices" by Pres. Thomas S. Monson -April 2016-found on lds.org

During one of my first chemo sessions, I briefly sat across from a girl who looked like she was about my age. She had no hair, and she was pale with a large pink burn we could see over half her neck and lower jaw. She had just finished radiation and could barely talk because her mouth sores were so painful. I feared that this would be me in the near future. I felt afraid and anxious. Many times, I gave into fear, but more often, I moved forward. Later, looking back, I realize how hard that year had been. Cancer is awful. Cancer treatment is awful, but who says that life is about ease?

When facing a challenge, you go toward it expecting to get hurt, but knowing that the pain is worth the reward. I once went to a self-defense class. The instructor told us that when you fight, you must expect to get hurt. Ultimately, the winner of the fight is the one that just won't stay down. What does winning look like in life? The scars, bruises, pain, and suffering do not define a loss. The spirit within can keep faith, stand strong, and remain devoted to truth despite what we may think we see on the surface. Being alive does not necessarily mean that we are winning, and dying does not mean someone has lost their battle either. Overcoming natural mortal tendencies and staying in control of who we are at the core, as children of God—that is winning. Winning is victory over our own weaknesses. Winning is taking the hits one after another, while still remaining firm and standing tall.

I wish people would stop saying someone has lost their battle with cancer when they die. I'd say they won their battle if they remained true and strong while living. They won their battle, but lost their life - there is a difference. Life is temporary but courage, strength, faith, and resiliency is eternal, and it should be congratulated in death. Compassion for everyone would be so much easier if we could see their victories won, but we cannot, so let's be kind anyway. Let's love anyway. Let's care when no one else does. We are all fighting for something.

I was blessed with an affliction that could be seen, but when the visual reminder of illness is removed and all that is left are the scars and pains of a battle once fought, the next battle begins. I will pick up the pieces and start over again with the new me. I must choose each day to not let cancer rule my life. I must choose every day what person I am that day. I pray to be the best version of me that I can. When I fall short, which I often do, and see the worst of myself, I can start over again, because I choose life. I choose trusting Grace for a self that will never be enough on my own. With God, all things are possible. Spend some time today looking at yourself, your true self. Are you doing what you want to be doing? Are you working right now, on becoming the person your creator wants you to become? If you are not moving in the direction you want to be going, then stop, turn around, and start running the right way!

We spend too much of our lives dedicated to things that don't matter. We should be gifting time to the things that do matter: our relationship with Deity, with self, with others, and our pursuit of true eternal happiness. If we're not working on that, then what exactly are we living for?

In early spring, when the snowdrifts are still melting and mornings are still bitter cold, my heart warms at the sight of dozens of crocuses fighting through the elements to offer a colorful greeting to the world. I don't know why or how such a small thing can fight through the snow and cold when much bigger plants shrink into the earth, waiting for a warmer spring.

Pain and suffering are just tools used to refine and strengthen us, to prepare us for the eternity to come. We are small and insignificant to the world like the little crocus peeking out of the snow, but my baby has proven to me that miracles often come in small packages.

The crocus reminds me to not underestimate the improbable. In a year of tears and uncertainty, my chemo baby was my glimpse of hope, and my grounding balance in chaos. He was my fifth C-section, but my first baby that I was allowed to hold right after delivery. Miracles surrounded him.

As cancer treatments ended and many of the side effects subsided, it became easier to let go of the anxiety that cancer brings. Normalcy returned. Then there were times, even months after completing treatments, that something would trigger fear. When driving to run errands with the music volume up loud, I would frequently cry. I was reminded of all of the times, parked on the side of the road, singing out my pain during treatments. Talking to new people about my story would make me cry, but the more I talked, the easier talking became. The more I wrote about my story, the less weight I felt on my shoulders.

Recovery takes one day at a time.

26 May 2016

One gift that cancer has given Brett and me is perspective: a desire to put aside non-essential expectations to make way for God's plan for us. We are moving 650 miles away tomorrow. We thought we would forever live in Utah. This has been our home since we met eleven years ago, and we have loved our time here. Another gift cancer has shown us is that without family, we are weak. We have relied so much on the generosity of others and have been grateful, but it has been humbling.

Over Christmas we visited with family in Arizona. At different times, Brett and I each felt a strong pull to stay. We, at different times and through different experiences, heard the whispering of the Holy Ghost confirm to us the feeling of home and peace in Arizona. We knew it was where our family needs to be. So, within two weeks of being back in Utah we discussed our impressions with each other and chose to put our trust in the Lord and His plans for us. Brett was given the opportunity to stay with his company and work remotely. We sold our home within two days of listing it, another tender mercy. We found our forever home in Arizona through a FaceTime call with our realtor.

The truck is almost all packed, the house is almost all cleaned, and I am almost all finished with my last Herceptin infusion and x-ray in Utah. We trust that this move is exactly what we need to be doing right now. Everything else will fall into place.

8 June 2016

We've arrived, unpacked a lot, and settled the kids into swim lessons and church activities. I've spent a total of three hours today in doctors' offices beginning with a pre-operative ultrasound with my new Ob/GYN before my kids' swim lessons. This afternoon I came to my new oncologist, which is where I am now. While waiting to see my doctor, I started tackling a puzzle in the waiting area. Do puzzles infuriate you as much as they do me? Why in the world would someone take a nice picture and cut it up into a thousand pieces and sell it as a game? And why do we buy them or do them, for free!? Maybe it's the satisfaction of seeing something broken and having the power to fix it. Maybe it's our innate desire to create that empowers us to see something beautiful out of the pieces.

Wouldn't it be sad if all we looked at were the pieces individually: the colors, the shapes, the edges, and never went beyond that discovery? One piece makes no sense. One piece is not a beautiful scene, a piece of art, or masterpiece. It is just one piece.

Today is just one day. A tantrum is just a tantrum. A broken vase is just a broken vase. A spill is just a spill. Cancer is just cancer. We can choose to spend all of our energy and emotion dedicated to one "piece" of our lives, or we can step back and look at it as a piece in a much bigger masterpiece that God has created. It may be one of the first pieces or it may be the last piece, but it is just a piece.

We all encounter "pieces" in our lives that seem to dangle right in front of our eyes. We can't see beyond it or around it. It takes up all of our energy and time. But a time will come when that piece over our eye is removed and we can hold it out and realize that it wasn't as big as we thought. The shape seems small, now that we can see it clearly from a distance, connecting perfectly to the rest of the pieces.

15 June 2016

There comes a time in every relationship where you have to unload your baggage and let it sit out while everyone around you decides where to put it all. Moving to a new state has me frequently asking myself when is a good time to "unpack." Unpack all at once, and it may scare people off or leave them feeling uncomfortable. Wait too long, and it will make for even more uncomfortable conversations of people feeling bad that they didn't know about my baggage.

I really don't care if people know that I'm near the end of cancer treatments. What I do want to avoid is making people feel uncomfortable to talk to me. We often go silent when someone is suffering, because we just don't know how to best respond. I do the same thing. "Here, have a meal. I'll stay as far away from you as possible because I don't want to offend you, hurt you, take up your time, etc."

So, here I am in a new place, wanting to make new friends, but unsure of how to not be awkward. "Hi! I'm Stephanie. I have five boys. I like to craft, write, watch movies, do projects of all kinds. Oh, and my hair is short because last year I was cancer bald, while pregnant. Yes, baby is fine. I'm going in for surgery next month to have all of my lady parts removed. So, what do you do for fun?" Maybe I need to work on my conversation skills. Or, maybe I'll just wait a little longer before I unpack. Emotional procrastination is the best kind.

5 July 2016

This morning I went to Costco with my three and four-year-olds. While in the parking lot I was grabbing my wallet and shutting doors when I saw my three-year-old run past the cars. I yelled, "FREEZE! STOP!" He didn't. He ran right across the parking lot all the way to the entrance of the store before I could catch him. He could have been hit by a car, but he wasn't.

An hour or so after we got home the kids were playing quietly in their room and I was folding laundry in my room. I walked into one of the boys' rooms to find my eleven-month-old with a Lego in his mouth and five more tiny pieces in his hand. He could have died choking, but he didn't.

Last night we went swimming (and we will again tonight), and at any moment someone could have drowned, but they haven't.

We shot off fireworks last night and I let my three-year-old do sparklers with his brothers. He could have thrown it onto someone and they would have been burned instantly, or it could have started a fire, but that didn't happen either.

We fill every day of our lives with risks. Risks that could be fatal to our fragile existence. We make choices, and sometimes those choices hurt us. Sometimes they don't. Sometimes the exact same choice one person makes will have a completely different effect on someone else. Some people get sick when they eat certain foods, but that doesn't stop me from eating. Some people are healed in miraculous ways, while others aren't.

This morning I read someone's remarks to one of my fellow cancer mommas. They were judgmental of her food choices because she has cancer, and the remarks were hurtful to my friend. I know that many times people are wanting to be helpful, but please be kind. Know that not everyone has the same life experiences, knowledge, or beliefs as you. We are all different and choose things that we feel are right, led by our own moral compass and how we see the world through our own lens of experiences.

When the goal is to sincerely help another, then we should do so with love and compassion, not forced guilt or shame. One person's cure can be another person's poison. One person's fact can be another person's fable. When in doubt, just love people. Love them because that's the best thing we can do for them and for ourselves. Lead them and guide them as needed, but love them first. When someone gets hurt, sick, or afflicted in some way just remember that any one of us could have the same thing happen. When people are suffering, we can help, mourn with them, and comfort them, but a time of pain is not a time to point fingers of shame.

19 July 2016

Quick update: I had my last Tamoxifen yesterday morning. I need to be off medicine for one week prior to surgery. My two oldest boys will be heading to camp this weekend. They were accepted into the Camp Kesem family! This non-profit camp is dedicated to giving children their childhood when cancer has touched their lives through a parent or close family member. They make a fun and safe environment to share feelings about difficult things, among peers and people who understand. Although my boys seem well adjusted, I am certain that there is buried fear that they hold onto.

I'll have my baby bearer removed next Tuesday (radical hysterectomy: hysterectomy, bilateral oophorectomy, and removal of cervix). We planned the surgery to be when my oldest boys will be gone so they won't worry. School starts a week after that. As for right now, I'm enjoying a good snuggle on the couch with my four-year-old while we watch Star Wars. Did I mention our miracle baby is walking now? I can't wait to celebrate his first birthday, but that's a good two and a half weeks away. Life moves on, thankfully.

26 July 2016

Prophylactic radical hysterectomy, here I come!

Why?

My triple positive breast cancer is highly hormone fed

Remove the hormones and starve the cancer

I've been medically inducing menopause for a while

This removal will allow me to get off the harsh medications that shut   down my ovaries

The female body receives the most hormones through the ovaries

Removal of both ovaries is called a bilateral oophorectomy

Ironically, one of the possible long-term side effects of Tamoxifen (my daily pill) is uterine cancer, nice huh? So, I've weighed my risks and rewards and decided to have it all removed

The second biggest hormone producer in the body is fat

I had no idea that fat actually did something other than make my pants tight

After surgery, I'll be off Tamoxifen and then my doc can switch my drugs to a fat hormone blocker, which has a higher rate of long term survival

PS are you wondering why there are no periods in this post? Take a moment to think about that

27 July 2016

Home is a great place to be. Brett says my stomach looks like I got in a knife fight. I think it looks more like shrapnel. Truthfully, they are cuts made by a robot, laparoscopically removing organs, but that just sounds too science fiction to me. Either way, they're cool scars.

28 July 2016

I'm already back at the cancer center for my every three-week infusion. Yes, two days after surgery. There is only one more infusion left! I can't wait to be finished! I got to meet someone new here by asking, "What are you in for?" I love meeting new cancer people, although I wish we met under different circumstances.

31 July 2016

"Is this hard to watch?" my seven-year-old asked me as I wiped tears from my face. We were watching a great show called Random Acts where cast members perform secret acts of service to unsuspecting people. The subject of service was a mom with Stage 4 breast cancer. She had just finished her fifth chemo treatment.

"When I was going through treatment I would have walked out, because it was too hard to watch any programs showing people with cancer. Now I feel like I can watch these shows, but I still cry sometimes," I responded.

"Are you sad crying or happy crying?" he asked.

"Good question. I'm sad/happy crying. I'm crying because I'm so happy to not be where she is right now. I'm so happy to be snuggling you and almost finished with treatment. I'm sad because I know where she is and I know how challenging her life is right now. I remember how hard it was when I was having chemo."

"One of my friends at camp had a mom with the same cancer as you but she died, and I met someone whose dad died from cancer."

"Does that make you sad?"

"Kind of. It makes me sad for them."

"That's called empathy, and that's a special gift to feel sad for someone who is sad too. Having empathy makes it easier to help people and to be a better friend."

I thank Camp Kesem for opening up a dialogue about a "heavy" topic in a carefree environment where kids can feel comfortable and safe opening up to talk. My two oldest boys had the privilege of going to camp last week and have already started asking when they can go back.

5 August 2016

I'm so excited! My doctor made me promise I wouldn't lift anything over ten pounds for at least ten days after surgery. My seven-year-old went to get the baby out of his crib this morning, as he has been doing since my surgery. Now, ten days later post-surgery, I happily stopped him and let him know that it was my turn! Mornings shouldn't start with tears, but I have to admit that I'm happy crying today. I can hold my baby! Just in time for his birthday this weekend!

7 August 2016

For the first six months of Brett Jr's life, he was fed by the generosity of ten women who donated what I could not give. These women selflessly and generously accumulated thousands of ounces of breastmilk, which they donated to Brett Jr. Their overproduction was a gift from Heaven. I never asked, but Heaven sent these angels to provide. They came and delivered over and over again. I don't feel like I can celebrate his birthday without celebrating the "milk maids" who nourished him exclusively for his first six months.

Because of sickness, surgeries, and chemo, I held him less than all my other kids. I hope to make that up to him over time. His friends in sixth-grade might make fun of him when I carry him to class on the first day of school. Okay, maybe I won't be that crazy, but I know I'll cry on his first day of kindergarten. He will always be my baby. He will always be my miracle. I am grateful every day that he saved my life. He is a blessing to our home and our family. Happy birthday to my Miracle Chemo Baby.

14 August 2016

Pain is pain. Suffering is suffering. Grief is grief. They may be handled in different ways, and the degree and situation may vary, but we can understand each other through these unifying emotions. Whether we are suffering from financial instability, depression, or even just a broken dish, we can be reassured that we are not alone. In a society of filters and Photoshop, sometimes we need to be reminded what is real, and what is real is what has no disguise, no pretense, no condition.

Our loving Father in Heaven has blessed us with people, lots of people. Reach out to love and serve. Look up to see what is around you. You may feel a piece of His love in the kind words of a friend or in the hug of your spouse, or the smile from a neighbor. Real relationships and real lives aren't always perfect. Real can be messy, but beautiful.

The world owes you nothing, but you owe it to yourself to become who God intended you to be. Be grateful, stop filtering what is real, vent when you need to vent, love more, fight less. Embrace pain as an equalizer to humankind. Don't hide behind pain or pretend like it's not there. We spend the majority of our time, money, and energy on things that just are not important. When it comes down to our purpose and destiny in life, we shy away from it, we are distracted from it, or we belittle our divinity. I am a child of God and He has sent me here. You are a child of God and He has sent you here. Pain, grief, and sorrow are temporary and an earthly affliction, not a Heavenly mandate. This is our reality.

19 August 2016

Once I had delivered the baby, I started getting Herceptin infusions every three weeks at the cancer center. Herceptin blocks the HER2 hormones and decreases recurrence of triple positive breast cancer. That makes six infusions of Adriamycin/ Cytoxin, a.k.a. The Red Devil,

four infusions of Taxotere, and NINETEEN infusions of Herceptin over a sixteen-month period. Today is my last one! This will be the last time they access my port. Next month I will finally get to say goodbye during my "de-Port-ation" surgery. Yay! I think I'll celebrate with ice cream and maybe a lively game of pin the chemo on the mutated cell. There's an empty infusion bag and a nice loud bell to ring and say goodbye to the infusion center and hello to a new start!

14 September 2016

One week until my last surgery! I had to remind myself to not take my medication this morning, because I'm supposed to be off of it for seven days before going into surgery. I am nervous and a bit anxious like I usually am before surgery. I've been contacted by a few people over the past week who have someone they love who has received a cancer diagnosis. They ask me what they can do to help. As usual, I send a list of things that will help with chemo or surgery to make things more comfortable or something that is helpful with side effects.

Last night, as I was thinking about my upcoming surgery, I thought of one important thing that I managed to neglect in the list of helps I had just sent: DON'T COUNT THEM OUT! Give them a week or a month to take in the news and figure things out, but after that first sting of mourning has passed, help them reach outside of themselves. A mind left wondering is dangerous for someone fighting for their life. Inevitably, the mind will take them to a dark place, yet the greatest cure for fear is selflessness.

During treatment, on my dark days, the Sunday School lesson that I needed to prepare for church helped me focus my mind on something other than myself. Sometimes going to church was hard. I would feel weak and would only make it for the one hour of my lesson and head straight back home to bed, but that lesson gave me courage. I remembered that cancer is temporary and faith in Jesus Christ is eternal. I know not everyone copes in the same way, but for me, I needed to keep my mind busy with something else so I didn't fall into darkness and fear. When I am stressed or worried and take on more projects, or volunteer to do more things, or do something that makes you wonder "why is she doing that when she should be focusing on something else," please just let me have that extra non-essential thing. The same could go for others fighting other battles.

Let the sick be sick, but when they want to not be sick and do something normal for once, let them be normal. Sometimes the best help you can give will be calling them up for advice on what jeans to buy, or recommendations for a great television series, or even calling them to complain about your own problems. The best thing you can do is make them feel like they are still them and they are still valuable.

21 September 2016

Here we go again. Finally having my exchange surgery where they will remove my tissue expanders and replace them with permanent implants. I'm also getting de-ported. I'm so happy to have that burrowing alien beetle device gone.

27 September 2016

Six days post-surgery, and I'm sitting in the waiting area to have my lab work done before I see the oncologist. The first few days were the most painful, but the pain was all at the surface, so not too bad. This time, Brett said it looked like I had been beaten with a baseball bat, because the bruising was pretty bad. I still have quite a bit of bruising, but that is getting better.

For the reconstruction surgery, I would expect the pain to be primarily in the chest, but not so. During the procedure, they do some fat grafting. The grafting consists of performing liposuction on my belly and transferring the fat to fill in pockets in my chest and armpit. The pain post liposuction not only looks like it but feels like getting hit by a baseball bat. I wear a compression belt around my waist 24/7 for another week, and it is uncomfortable and hot. I'm just SO glad it's cooling down in Arizona now, so I'm not wearing this in 110 degree weather.

The pain isn't noticeable now unless I bend over to pick something up or get bumped in the waist. I stopped taking pain meds last week and I really don't think I've needed them, except for a few days ago when my three-year-old accidentally head-butted me in the belly (not too hard, luckily). I immediately went to my knees in pain and just kneeled down for about five minutes while my boys continued to play tag around me. Then I got back up just fine and told them I would be out for the next round. Every morning, I wake up feeling better than I did the day before.

Summary: Life is good. Lipo is bad. Don't play tag after surgery. That's all.

23 December 2016

We wrap presents for Christmas, taking care with each fold of the wrapping paper to make the lines smooth before we stack the gifts away to come out on Christmas Eve. Wrapping the presents in colorful fun paper is such a great tradition, where the real gift is hidden from the receiver's eyes. When the boys see the colorful paper and carefully taped tags and ribbons, their imagination will soar with curiosity. Then, in just a couple of days, they will be able to tear through that paper. The simple paper that promised something amazing inside is tossed in excitement for the intended gift hiding beneath.

We have so many gifts in our lives that we don't recognize because the wrapping may not be as shiny, or tied with a bow.

Sometimes it's through the greatest pain that we are able to see the greatest gifts given to us. Cancer is the greatest pain of my life, but it is also my greatest gift. This Christmas, I have so many reasons to fall on my knees to worship Jesus. He is the embodiment of our faith. He is the proof that Heavenly Father hears our prayers and answers them. The world rejoices at His coming still, because by and through Him we are healed and free, because we are His.

I felt the greatest peace and contentment when I internalized that my eternal nature and immortal existence in the world to come was far greater than any imagined expectation of what my life is or could be. Though our choices now pull a great weight in eternity, the time here is so small. It's up to us to shrink in the battle or take the beatings with pride. This is a small moment.

12 February 2017

Brett told me a couple of weeks ago that he had volunteered our family to do a special musical number for sacrament meeting. My first thoughts went something like this: "Have you met our kids? Are you crazy? Do we have to? Can I hide?"

After talking to the kids about it and discussing it together, we agreed that Brett would sing a song with the three oldest boys. I would handle the two youngest so there would not be mass chaos. I also saw it as an excuse for me to not have to sing with them and be the only female voice.

They practiced, and our three-year-old surprisingly wanted to sing as well. We managed to get everyone healthy after a crazy vomit-filled week, AND we managed to have everyone dressed with matching socks and combed hair (we were missing the baby's shoes, but oh well), AND we arrived at the chapel a few minutes early.

The time came. They clumsily tripped over all the toys, notebooks, and scriptures lining the floor and pew where our family sat to make their way to the front of the congregation. I sat with the baby and their Partridge grandparents who came to watch. Brett and the four boys stood nicely in front of the microphone. Just as the piano was starting to play, my five-year-old, O-Man, looked straight at me and said loudly enough for me to hear, "Mom, I'm standing on a stool!" Then they began to sing, and my ever so rambunctious, sometimes awful to get along with, three-year-old started blowing a dozen kisses at me while they sang. I cried. I smiled. The singing wasn't perfect, the boys didn't remember all the words, but they sang. Brett did a great job of carrying the tune for everyone.

When the song ended, my five-year-old announced to the congregation in excitement that he saw his friend. A few other things were said into the microphone from the sweet high-pitched voices of my third and fourth sons, who didn't seem to notice the congregation hearing each word. It was all beautiful. My family isn't perfect and truthfully sometimes they make me crazy, but I love them. I love that they play board games together on Sunday and almost always build forts with our couch. I love that every fight, which they have a lot of, is always worked out or forgotten by the time we sit to eat dinner. I love that my crazy toddler sings "I Am a Child of God" to the baby almost every day when I put him to bed. I love that they can tell each other knock, knock jokes that don't make any sense and still laugh. Today they sang "I Love to See the Temple," and it made me so happy and grateful to know that this crazy, sweet, bickering, noisy, messy, helpful, obnoxious pack of boys are mine forever. I'll take it, happily. My life is blessed.

Chapter Ten

-The Reflection-

Brett and I noticed something was awry with our oldest son when he was in preschool. He struggled holding still and focusing during class. We practiced the alphabet and sight words from the time he was three, yet he still didn't recognize letters consistently. He wasn't able to read beginner words even into the first grade. We hired a reading tutor and began seeing some progress, but he frequently complained of headaches and dreaded reading.

Through a tender mercy, we heard about vision disorders and had him tested by a specialist. Somehow, in his seven years of life, we had never noticed that he was unable to cross his eyes, which is an essential part of being able to read. The doctor diagnosed him with vision convergence disorder.

With months of attentive vision therapy each day, his doctor was able to train our son's eye muscles to converge properly. When therapy had completed, it only took about a year and a half to be caught up to grade level reading standards. He now loves to read. I can't imagine how his life would have been different had he never been able to converge his eyes to see words on a page.

Fast forward three years, while we were eating lunch together. Our son started talking about a cyclops he had recently read about in a book. This conversation was a welcome topic over the flatulence or video game discussions that usually occur around the dining table. He explained that a cyclops could not have good vision, because it only has one eye. This led to a discussion about why our two eyes working together give us greater ability to focus and a wider range of vision.

As we cleaned off the table from lunch, I began to reflect on how my life has changed since cancer blessed my life. I used to see my life in a one-dimensional way. I had a mindset of letting life happen to me each day. My direction could accurately be described as horizontal stagnancy. I was a bit frazzled, but happy. I was oblivious to pain, but content. I was Heavenly hopeful, but going nowhere.

To be horizontally stagnant was living each day like the last. There were no upward ambitions or even a realization that each day was the same as the last. The children were growing but our family unity was not. I felt like I was at the limit of my ability to maintain sanity as a parent. I did not know that I was barely scratching the surface of my ability to handle stressful circumstances.

Cancer pushed me beyond what I thought were my limitations, and forced me to face my fears and doubts. Cancer pushed me beyond what I thought was the limit of my pain and stress. Cancer pushed and pushed again, each time making me feel weaker. During this weakened state, I fell to my knees and reached up to my God. I was weak, but I knew He was strong. I was afraid, but I knew that His love could overpower fear. An ancient prophet once boldly proclaimed to his son that, "...perfect love casteth out *all fear*" (The Book of Mormon, Moroni 8:16). Love is stronger than fear and God's love for me was the perfect love that I needed to allow into my heart.

When it comes to our spiritual understanding of our mortality and our relationship with our Heavenly Father, we are kind of like a cyclops. We see things linearly, while God sees things from every direction, in an eternal circular loop. His vision of truth which does not deviate or become crooked, allows Him to be the same yesterday, today, and forever. When we align our linear views with His eternal perspective, we find a balance that can bring us peace and joy.

Like my son's vision disorder, we can suffer from an emotional or spiritual convergence disorder that prohibits us from seeing things as they really are. Our limited views can cause us to narrowly make false assumptions about our pain and our heartache, lacking real depth of understanding. Although my spiritual vision is not perfect, I believe that cancer humbled me to see my nothingness, weakness, and need for total dependence on others and God. My Father in Heaven helped me see things clearly when I allowed Him to show me what I could not see and what I could not understand. I needed to let go of my perception of reality and let God fill in what I could not understand.

When I was in my darkest hours, I felt as though the world was falling to rubble around me. I believed that my body was defective and failing. I learned that expectations can fail, plans can fail, ambitions can fail, even people can fail, but the pure love of Christ cannot and will not fail. We are not left alone, and we are not left comfortless. God does not falter, and when we cling to Him, the world can fall around us, our bodies can even fail us, but we will be secure in the arms of His perfect grace.

I can watch the delicate wings of a butterfly and admire the beauty, knowing their life is short, but their purpose is fulfilled, and I see God's hand. I see God in the details of nature: the sun reflecting off a speck of dust, the sound of thunder roaring from a distance, the vision of hope glistening in the eyes of a child, and the ever-present hum of the living earth carrying us each day. The Father of earth and Heaven carefully and thoughtfully orchestrates beauty and order in the midst of chaos. Stop. Look up. Look outside yourself and you may see pain or even death as a friend, offering passage to a welcome embrace back to the home where we all began. It was when I became at peace with the possibility of my death that I truly was able to let go and live. Whatever happens in the now or in the future, I am at peace.

I am a different person now that cancer has changed me. I am really living. I don't know that I could fully comprehend what living meant until the option of life was in question. Living is about taking charge and ownership of my choices. Living is about making things happen instead of waiting for things to happen. Living is about knowing when to stop the dispensable aspects of the day and take a moment to grasp onto the sacred truths and eternal relationships that surround us. Living is about taking risks, giving hope, and finding joy in the journey. I embrace life, but I am not afraid of dying.

Brett and I went on our ten-year anniversary cruise, albeit a year and a half late. It was difficult to say goodbye to the kids when we left. When I got over my homesickness, the vacation was just what I needed, just what we needed.

During one of the port stops, we went to a local beach to enjoy the sand and sea. Brett went to swim in the ocean after sitting on the beach for a while. The waves hitting the beach were not big, but strong. I followed suit and began swimming. The water was warm and pleasant. After a few minutes, I saw that Brett was far away. Without realizing it, I had been caught in a current that was pulling me farther and farther away. I began to panic when my attempts to get to Brett or to shore were futile. My arms and legs were exhausted in a matter of minutes. I looked to the shore where dozens of people were playing in the sand, drinking, and sun bathing. I was drowning, surrounded by people, and no one could see me. I managed to get out of the current, but my energy was completely spent as I attempted to get to shore. A wave pushed me to the beach where I crashed into the sand and tried to get to my knees. Another wave beat me into the sand. Brett and our friends ran to help me up and get me away from the water. After some coughing up water and resting, it was as though nothing wrong had happened. I was fine and laughing about it five minutes after the ordeal. We continued to have a great vacation.

When faced with pain, grief, or insurmountable burdens, we may feel like we are drowning. We may look around, feeling completely alone in our afflictions. We may be comparing our misery with another's perceived perfection. We may feel like the Picasso in a Michelangelo gallery: misunderstood, appearing broken, and out of place.

No matter our ailment, and no matter how deep we are in the darkness, there is always help, hope, and someone who can understand. The prideful attitude of taking one's pain without help is denying the power and strength that comes from support. Whenever you feel like you are drowning, know that someone does see you. Someone is ready and wanting to give you a hand or direct you to help. You may not see them, but help is there. You are not alone. You are not invisible, but it may take a shout for help to sound the alarm for rescue to come.

While we cleaned the dishes cleared from the table, my third son came running in with mismatched clothes and unkempt hair, the chocolate smeared all over his face only magnified his mischievous smile. He asked if he could have some more M&Ms. I looked at him and grinned. Dirty dishes, laundry, dirty handprints on windows, and the ever-present drumming of feet running from one side of the house to another: this is my present. I lose my temper and patience at times, but when the house is quiet and the boys are all asleep, I ponder on all that is and was. I walk into my boys' bedrooms while they sleep, picking up toys left on the floor, and tucking their blankets tight around them. This crazy mess is my amazing, beautiful, and blessed life.

Please consider leaving a review on
Amazon and Goodreads.
Thank you!

Keep reading for useful notes and tips!

About Cancer

Cancer is an uncontrolled division of abnormal cells, usually contained within a set part of the body. Most cancers form into a cancerous mass or tumor, but there are some cancers, like leukemia, that divide and spread without forming a mass and without a specified origin. There are many different types of cancer, and each person (having their own individualized genetic makeup) will find that there are many different ways to treat their particular cancer. We use the generalized term chemotherapy to describe the medicine(s) given to destroy fast growing and fast multiplying cells. There is no one magic chemo drug to eradicate all cancers. There are several individual medicines and concoctions that could be used to treat a person's cancer, but simply calling it all chemotherapy is easier.

Some cancers don't need chemo and can be treated by removing the mass, administering radiation, and/or oral prescriptions. Some chemo drugs have milder side effects while others are severe.

If you are recently diagnosed with cancer, you will be inundated with doctors' appointments and more information than you could possibly process. You may also have a period of mourning that can make remembering important details difficult. Record everything! It will help you in the long run, I promise. Even when you think some things are too obvious to forget, write it down anyway. Write down what each doctor says along with all diagnoses and procedures. I haven't been perfect at this, but I am so glad for the notes I have kept in my planner.

Doctors are wonderful and they do their best to coordinate with each other. As a general rule, you should not put your life and health haphazardly in someone else's hands. A panel of doctors doesn't sit around for hours on end at a discussion table to help you alone (despite what you may think from watching hospital dramas on TV); they have a lot of other people to worry about as well. I am so glad I don't have to carry the stress of being a doctor!

Your oncologist has one very important job: kill cancer and keep you alive. Killing cancer is a big job and they do it well. They will give you a packet with information about chemo side effects and the prescriptions to counteract them. They will do their best to provide you with information and resources, but their job is not to ensure that you make it back to work a day after chemo.

Your health and wellness is your own responsibility. Learn all you can, pray hard, and get help from people who can help. Chemo runs its course through your body and the effects can often stay with you for years to come and even a lifetime. You may want to see a dietician, a chiropractor, a dentist, a psychologist, etc. The more extra help you get, the better you will feel.

In October 2015, I dedicated the month to answering questions about cancer on my Facebook page. The questions were sincere and I hope the answers are informative and beneficial to both people with cancer and those just curious. These notes are a great resource to find answers and tips, taken directly from my posts during Breast Cancer Awareness Month.

What should I expect on a Chemo Day?

Here is a detailed play-by-play of MY chemo treatment. Different cancer centers, doctors, and treatments may have different routines and protocol.

One hour prior to my scheduled infusion appointment I rub lidocaine over my port (some use a spray lidocaine). This will numb the area in preparation for the port needle. At my first treatment, I put way too much cream on my port. It smeared all over my shirt by the time I got to the cancer center. I learned you should put a small piece of plastic on top of the lidocaine (Saran Wrap is great) to keep it from seeping onto clothing. Also, be sure to wash your hands after application unless you want numb hands.

Arrival at cancer center: Front row parking is my favorite! I can only speak for my own experience, but I hope all medical centers have prime parking for cancer patients.

Check in: Right after checking in, I get weighed and then led to a patient room where they take my vitals. After vitals are taken, they access the port, which just means they wipe off the lidocaine with alcohol and then jab the port with the needle that will be connected to the IV (I never watch). They flush out the port and draw blood to be tested. I wait, but it doesn't take too long.

Meeting with the doctor: Once the lab results are in, the oncologist comes into the patient room. He goes over the results. Red and white blood counts are good, slightly anemic, etc. He listens to my breathing and my heart and then I lie down and he pushes on my stomach in several areas. His main concern is checking for tenderness, pain, or abnormal masses that would indicate cancer spreading, especially in the liver. After I'm given the all clear I pull out my list of questions I've written in my notes. I always have questions. We go through each concern and discuss the facts.

Off to the infusion room: I get to pick which recliner to sit in (I always cross my fingers for one of the two comfiest chairs). Once I sit in my seat, I start to make myself at home. I pull out my chemo bag, which I think is a must for treatment. Here's what I pack:

- Soft blanket- I get cold during infusion, so some kind of blanket or Snuggy is a must.

- Ice packs- Mine are homemade in quart Ziploc bags. I use six ice packs while they infuse the Taxotere. I feel like I'm in slight hypothermia when I do this. My hands and feet become numb so after time the cold doesn't bother me as much. Icing helps prevent neuropathy. Not all chemos cause neuropathy, but if it does I highly recommend this process.

- Tablet and headphones- The cancer center has Wi-Fi. Once I've settled in and talked with my other cancer friends in the seats next to me, I turn to Netflix. A mindless show that distracts me without making my brain work too hard is a great way to pass time. I never forget my headphones either!

- Cold green smoothie- goodness from my favorite local smoothie bar. This is my favorite chemo day tradition with my husband.

• Gum- A lot of people also bring hard candies. Having something yummy to chew or drink is great. Many people get the taste of the infusion in their mouth and it is atrocious. I've only experienced that once, luckily.

• Frozen grapes- Although I didn't have them today, I usually bring them to chew on during Taxotere to prevent mouth sores.

• Warm comfy socks are a must!

• A friend!- Some people sit alone, but most have someone with them during their infusion. It makes all the difference knowing that someone is there with you who has your back. Having a person close to keep an eye on you in case you have a reaction to one of the drugs is also practical. They can quickly call a nurse for assistance when needed.

• A book crossword, or Sudoku are nice

• Chapstick- Dry mouth is annoying and common.

• Cell phone

• A smile- A great attitude is always healing.

Being Home: For the first few hours my body feels strange. The feeling is not painful or nauseating at first. The feeling can be compared to when your body is trying to fall back into place after getting off a roller coaster. It fades. I still get to see my kids when they get home from school, help with homework, run errands, put kids to bed, and walk a few miles on the treadmill.

Cancer doesn't stop the world from spinning or dishes from needing to be washed. Cancer is not easy, and sometimes recovery is harder and slower than you expect, but life goes on-thankfully. Chemo day is done!

What Causes Cancer?

Parabens, sulfates, iodine deficiency, obesity, malnutrition, hairspray, cooking spray, wheat, meat, negative attitude, MSG, processed soy, plastic, lotion, fluoride, microwaves, pesticides, milk, cigarettes, food coloring, paint, estrogen, testosterone, not having children, having children, not breastfeeding, pollution, cell phones, too much sun, not enough sun, tobacco, genetics. . .

I hope you recognize how sarcastic I am being. I could go on and on with this list. There are endless amounts of things that have been labeled as *cancer causing*. Only some of those are proven to contribute to cancer growth. Some people have it, some people don't. Everybody reacts to the environment around them differently, so what hurts one person may have no effect on another.

I have known very healthy people diagnosed with cancer, and I've also known some remarkably unhealthy people who live long "healthy" lives. I'm NOT saying that there's no point in trying to be healthy because there is! We should do all we can to help ourselves, but we shouldn't blame ourselves for things that are out of our control.

I recently read an article whose author claimed to know the cause of cancer. After a lengthy investigation of many common foods and household products, the study basically concluded that being alive causes cancer, just like I asserted above. Mutations like freckles, dimples, birthmarks, and long second toes: these are reminders that we are all mutants, although some mutations are cooler than others and only some try to kill us.

It can be overwhelming trying to free yourself from all unhealthy foods and practices, all while adding in all that is good for your body to be healthy. I'm not going to give you a fix-all easy solution, because there aren't any, but here are some specific baby steps that will help keep you healthier.

Iodine Deficiency: In 1924 the Morton Salt Company developed iodized salt to prevent goiters, which were common ailments of the time. The FDA required they label the salt, "This salt provides iodine, a necessary nutrient." Shortly after this implementation, goiters in the US decreased dramatically. I started looking into this when I learned that several of my cancer buddies in one of my support groups were using an iodine supplement, so I asked my oncologist about it. Our bodies need iodine for our thyroid health, fetal development, and brain and nervous system functionality. The biggest source of iodine is sea vegetables (seaweed, kelp, etc.), milk, and iodized salt. If you're like me and don't drink milk or eat sea vegetables, then salt is really the best and often only source of iodine.

My oncologist said our bodies don't need much, and ensuring that we use iodized salt at home would be fine. I looked in my cupboard and realized under my salt label in small print it said, "Does not contain iodine, a necessary nutrient." Lame! I never thought about iodine before, but now I've taken this baby step to better my health by purchasing iodized salt. Himalayan Sea Salt is my first choice of natural mineral salt.

I believe in a key piece of wisdom that would benefit everyone's life in a number of ways: moderation in all things. A lot of fad diets out there don't have a leg to stand on because they aren't sustainable for a lifetime. By making small and simple steps to better health you can experience lasting effects.

I want to mention moderation first because there are beneficial things we can add to our diet for a healthier life, but excessive use of anything, even water, can be detrimental. Today's perfect example: soy. Soy is a beneficial bean for heart health and decreasing the risk of certain conditions. However, the studies originally proving these benefits were done on the whole bean. When the bean becomes cut up, processed, and altered, the health benefits are also altered and even mutated to become harmful.

When I was diagnosed, I first looked at my diet. I asked my oncologist's PA if there were any foods in particular that I should avoid or add to my diet. Her first response was to cut out soy. I thought that would be pretty easy, because I don't drink soy milk or eat tofu. Wrong! Soy particles are in just about EVERYTHING! Start reading your labels and you'll be shocked to find it in almost every processed product you consume in your day: cereal, granola bars, crackers, noodles, even peanut butter. It starts becoming scary when you realize how much soy you are actually consuming in a day. Soy is a cheap filler and studies are now showing that once processed, soy has some harmful cancer-causing effects. Beware of over consumption of any one thing (soy is one example, but this can be applied to many other things). Moderation in all things will give you a healthier, happier life.

While there is not one answer as to why some people get cancer, there are things that can be done to improve your health and help in the prevention of cancerous cells thriving within your body. The Mayo Clinic gives seven tips to reduce your risk of cancer:

1. Don't use tobacco.
2. Eat a healthy diet. *
3. Maintain a healthy weight and be physically active.
4. Protect yourself from the sun.
5. Get immunized.
6. Avoid risky behaviors.(I actually laughed when I saw this. Watch out! That looks risky! You might get cancer!

This is a very blanketed, vague tip, but there must be good reason for it.)

7. Get regular medical care.

("Cancer Prevention: 7 Tips to Reduce your Risk" 5 November 2015, MayoClinic.org)

* Eating a healthy diet can translate differently from one person to the next. For me, food has always been a way to not be hungry, and deliciousness to be enjoyed. That was it. It wasn't until cancer that I really started to see food as a tool and the "oil" to my body's machine. We all have to start somewhere and you alone can decide what your best fit will be for a diet plan. My diet has evolved many times, but cancer blessed me with a spiritual view of food.

Our Father in Heaven wants us to learn to trust Him and lean on the Savior for grace. To learn this, He has gifted us with families and communities, where we learn through experience how to forgive, love, show charity, and depend on others.

I believe that He has provided what we need in life to find joy and happiness, including creating this Earth for us. While we learn to be more charitable and love one another through our relationships, we often forget to utilize another partner provided for our success—the Earth. The more pure, whole foods we can add into our diet, the better, because that's what plants are here for. The Earth is here for us and what the Earth produces is for our good. These are our Father in Heaven's gifts to us: the Earth and everything on it. We should spend more of our lives appreciating these gifts by utilizing them on a daily basis. Eat less junk, less man-made manipulations, and more pure plant-based foods. I will not fully commit to one specific diet plan, but I will be certain that every day I get my Earth health support.

Because It's All About That Lump

I never thought I needed to do a breast self-exam until I was old. It never dawned on me that someone age thirty-two with no family history of breast cancer could even have cancer. You are NEVER too young to do a monthly self-exam. In fact, it is a huge benefit to start monthly exams when you are young so you can get in the habit and get to know what 'normal' feels like.

Make it a routine: first day of the month is self-exam day in the shower, or maybe first day of your period. Many people don't know what to look for, but if you are doing exams every month then you will likely know if something feels abnormal.

How did I know? Shortly after I found out I was pregnant my right breast became really sore. It felt EXACTLY like having a clogged milk duct. I had no reason to believe it was anything different. The soreness went away after a couple of days, but I could still feel the hardened lump. This is fairly abnormal to feel sudden pain associated with a cancer tumor. Cancer usually comes in slowly and unnoticed. It felt exactly like a marble beneath my skin, surrounded by tissue. After the pain subsided I thought it was strange that a small area was still hard, even a month after I noticed it.

At my 16-week pregnancy checkup with my OB/GYN I expressed my surprise to have a clogged milk duct so early in pregnancy. He ordered an ultrasound to have a closer look, and you know the rest of the story.

I hear too many stories of women like me that assume their lump is nothing. They don't address it until it is too late. I have also heard a lot of stories of doctors that have ignored lumps in patients because the patient is young or pregnant. They take the "let's wait and see if it goes away on its own" mentality. By the time these situations are caught, many women are already in advanced stages of breast cancer.

We shouldn't be paranoid, but this is where monthly exams are essential. If you are checking every month, you will notice if something feels different. My lump was obvious, but could clearly be misdiagnosed as a clogged milk duct. I know that my OB/GYN saved my life by having me get that ultrasound. Being pregnant super-charged my hormone fed cancer. We needed to shut down that all-you-can-eat buffet for cancer in my body.

If I had not had that ultrasound, I likely would have gone months before saying anything again. By that time it would have been too late. Know yourself. Know when to follow your gut, and get a second opinion if necessary. If you are over forty, of if you have a family history of cancer, get a yearly mammogram. This is your life, take charge of your health!

The Six Best Things To Give Someone Starting Chemotherapy:

1 Support and love: This is free and very much needed. Cancer can feel lonely. People tend to not know how to talk to people with cancer, or they stay away in an effort to not be a disturbance. Yes, a lot of times chemo patients will keep their distance by their own choice, but they want it to be *their* choice. Don't forget to invite them to things, send notes of encouragement, text and check in on them, etc. (I didn't put calling on the list because sometimes emotions are raw and talking on the phone can be hard.) Motivational pick-me-up cards or pictures to hang up around their home are great. These seemingly small gestures are a HUGE help. Then, if they are feeling well they can respond, but don't expect a response.

2 Food: This is one thing that made it on everyone's list of perfect gifts. I am blessed with an amazing church that took care of organizing meals for us many times so we didn't even have to think about it. We, and many other cancer patients, preferred freezer meals as gifts. Sometimes, you just don't know when it will be a good day or a bad day. Ready-to-go freezer meals are perfect. Be sure to ask if there are any special diet restrictions or preferences so that no good meal need be wasted.

3 Chemo Bag Gifts: Most people that are undergoing chemotherapy have a bag designated for bringing to chemo. They keep things in it to make them comfortable, distracted, and busy during their infusion. From the dozens of people I surveyed, here are some gift ideas that people recommend bringing during infusions: a small cooler, big water bottle, warm blanket, heating pad, pillow, all natural lip balm, good strong lotion (no scent), mints, a magazine, pretzels or trail mix, gum, beanie, fuzzy socks, Netflix or Hulu subscription, and/or a book.

4 Recovery Gifts: Cute pajamas (if they are having surgeries, go with button down), Biotene mouthwash, a nice thermometer, scarves, throw up bags, soft bristle toothbrushes, movies, or a silk pillowcase. If they have small children, then offering to watch kids is a huge help. You can also give gifts to the children like puzzles, treats, coloring books, games, etc. The kids need just as much love and support at this time as the parents.

5 Lifting the Burden Gifts: Many chemo patients will spend half their time being sick and the other half trying to enjoy their loved ones as much as possible. Taking care of some of the extra things is a great gift. The most mentioned service gifts were cleaning their home or donating money for a cleaning service and lawn work. Cancer treatments are expensive and for some, they are completely financially consuming. Gift certificates to a grocery store or a gas station are helpful. Some fighting cancer have charities you can donate to, helping with medical expenses. Before donating, be certain the charity is actually sponsored by a trustworthy source. When in doubt, send money directly to your intended recipient.

6 "What cancer?" Gifts: Another idea is to give them something to take a night "off" from cancer. Offering to watch kids and giving a gift certificate to a restaurant, movie theater, or sporting event is a fun way to show your support. Sometimes a night away from troubles can revive the soul.

Acknowledgements

Words, phrases, and sometimes paragraphs would come to my mind as glimpses of inspiration during my cancer treatments. I know that anything in this book that inspires, motivates, or strengthens your faith in God is not to my credit. Often the words came when *I* needed to hear them. The Holy Ghost spoke to my heart and mind and I simply recorded the message. I thank my Savior for healing my broken heart and sharing His peace in my chaos.

I give special thanks to my husband and extended Partridge and Rushton families for being a powerful source of strength and support. Thank you for picking up my slack and making me feel less like a patient and more like me - on sabbatical.

To my boys: Thank you for loving me unconditionally. You inspire me and I am honored to be your mother and friend. I hope someday you will understand the depth of my love for you.

To Dr. Ryan Jones, M.D.: You could have waived it off as a clogged milk duct, but you didn't. Thank you for being in tune with my needs and taking precaution on an unlikely cancer candidate. You were the start of my early detection. You saved my life and gave me the perfect delivery of our healthy baby. You will always hold a place in my heart.

Dr Cordell Bott M.D., Dr. Jennifer Tittensor M.D., Dr. Mark Jensen M.D., Dr. Brandon Barney M.D., Dr. Grayson Guzman M.D., Dr. Santosh Rao M.D., Intermountain Healthcare providers, American Fork Hospital, Revere Health, and Banner MD Anderson Cancer Center: Each of you have played a vital part of my treatment and recovery. Thank you for caring for me as a mother, wife, and friend– not just another patient. I knew that I was in the best hands and appreciate your work and expertise in saving lives and giving hope. You are my team, and your service will never be forgotten.

Thanks also goes to those who voluntarily helped read, edit, and critique my manuscript. If it were not for their honest recommendations, praise, and candid insights into improving this work, the entire book would be one, rather large, run on sentence (case in point). I am not a great writer, but they gave me the tools to keep going. After four re-writes, several additions and subtractions, together we made this book what it is today. Writing a book can now be checked off my bucket list.

Lastly, but definitely not least in my appreciation, I wanted to thank every person who cared for my children, brought over meals, mowed our lawn, donated breast milk, sent cards, and prayed for my family and me. Their influence and example has changed my life and taught me true Christ-like love and charity. I admire their selfless generosity. I have recorded each of their names in my journal of services given. Their acts of service are sacred to my family and we hold them dear to our hearts. For those who wish to remain anonymous, I honor their wishes. I offer my sincere gratitude and affection. Thank you.

About the Author:

Stephanie Rushton Partridge is a wife, mother, sister, daughter, crafter, baker, Amazon shopper, movie watcher, laundry doer, book writer, people observer, planner, wish maker, laptop worker, diaper changer, butterfly kisser, and thesaurus user.

Writing has been a healing therapy for her. She plans to write about other topics in the future. Breast cancer is a part of her identity, but it is not who she is.

In *Cancer Moms and Chemo Babies* Stephanie shares the detailed conversation she and Brett had with their children about her cancer diagnosis. The profits from Cancer Moms and Chemo Babies go to charity.

Thank you for reading Baby Bump, Cancer Lump. Please write a review on Amazon and/or Goodreads. Stephanie would be happy to answer questions about her experiences with cancer, share with you how writing can be a healing outlet, or show you how to write your own story. You can contact her at www.stephanierpartridge.blogspot.com or on Facebook at StephaniesPinkRibbon.

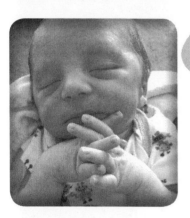

Recomended
Charitable
Organizations

Camp Kesem.org
Metavivor.org
HopeForTwo.org

Made in United States
Orlando, FL
13 April 2022

16821809R00112